cint c

CINE EAST
Hong Kong Cinema Through The Looking Glass

First edition published July 1998
by FAB Press

FAB Press, PO Box 178, Guildford, Surrey, GU3 2YU, England, U.K.
(email: harvey@fabpress.demon.co.uk)

Thanks to:
All those interviewed for their time, generosity, and assistance; Daisy Chu King Oi (for all the help
and encouragement, and transcribing the Johnnie To interview); David Bordwell; John Charles;
Stephen Cremin; Lai Chi Kai (Win's Group); Roger Lee (Harvest Crown Ltd); June Shum (Era); Li
Cheuk To; Media Asia; Rick Baker (Eastern Heroes); Janice (Milkyway Image); Maggie Tse; Maria
Koo (UFO concept); Joyce Cheung (Urban Coucil P.I.U.); I.C.A.; Jerry Tsang; CoCo; Marc Morris

Acknowledgements:
BOB & Partners; Brilliant Idea Group; China Star Entertainment Group; City Entertainment
Magazine; Film Workshop; Golden Harvest; Media Asia Films; Mei Ah; Ocean Shores International;
United Filmmaker Organization; Universe Films; Win's Entertainment; Michael Curtin, Richard
James Havis, Ming Pao Daily News, Harri Rampotti, Hong Kong International Film Festival.

Cover photographs:
front: *Lau Ching Wan in FULL ALERT*
back: *LOVING YOU*
Frontispiece:
Publicity shot for Andrew Lau's RAPED BY AN ANGEL

A CIP catalogue record for this book is available from the British Library

ISBN 0 9529260 2 4

The Author

Miles Wood studied film at Newcastle-Upon-Tyne Polytechnic, though the three year course didn't
include a single movie from Hong Kong. He believes the only reason the college tape library
included a copy of Sammo Hung's "The Victim" was that it was mistaken for the Dirk Bogarde
picture. His interest in Hong Kong cinema, about which he has written for various UK and US
publications, took him to the Special Administrative Region where he currently resides.
"Cine East" is his first book.

CINE EAST

Hong Kong Cinema Through The Looking Glass

Miles Wood

A
FAB
PRESS
PUBLICATION

狄龍 張曼玉
任達華 李子雄
劉錫明 許志安

監製 導演
林德祿

出品人 馬碧蓮　絕不低頭 FIRST SHOT　演出 周匡朝 張鳳妮 金興賢 江文瑩

contents

Preface: *by David Bordwell* 6

Introduction 8

FOREWORD

by David Bordwell

Hong Kong cinema has swept over Western film culture in two distinct waves. First, in the 1970s, martial arts movies introduced the world to a unique combat tradition and brought Bruce Lee and his contemporaries to international renown. Then in the late 1980s, Westerners met Jackie Chan, Tsui Hark, John Woo, Ching Siu-tung, Yuen Kuei, Kirk Wong, and others who showed what an invigorating, explosive action cinema could be. Thanks to enterprising film programmers and the global reach of video, Hong Kong cinema won a core of devotees and sidled into mainstream film culture. Now Michelle Yeoh partners with Pierce Brosnan, and Jackie Chan stars in Mountain Dew commercials.

Undeniably, however, some things have changed. Hong Kong's film industry has been in a slump since 1993. The local audience discovered other diversions, like karaoke and video games; video piracy made films available simultaneous with their theatrical release; and the regional market began to wither. American studios recruited major talents. Most recently, Hong Kong companies have been hit hard by the Asian economic crisis, which will force budgets lower and reduce the number of films made. Movie-making will be riskier than ever.

At the same time, you are starting to hear murmurs about the good old days. Today's action pictures, some say, seem listless compared to classics like **A Better Tomorrow** and **Once upon a Time in China**. And Chow Yun-Fat, the most bankable and charismatic local star, now brings his cool to the Hollywood backlot. Are the great days of this cinema over?

If a golden age has ended, it had an extraordinarily long run - from the fine early works of the New Wave (**Dangerous Encounters: First Kind** and **The Spooky Bunch**, both 1980) and the reinvigorated martial arts cinema (**Young Master**, 1980, and **Legendary Weapons of China**, 1982) through the extraordinary films of the mid-1980s to the daring accomplishments of the early nineties. Any country would be proud to have produced so many zany and zestful films in a dozen years of frantic output.

The interviews you are about to read cast new light on this remarkable era. They yield many insights into what gave 1980s cinema its unique energy. But another merit of this book is to show that Hong Kong moviemaking has moved into a mature phase.

One symptom of this is the emergence of Wong Kar-Wai in international festivals. Although Wong's local box office power is anemic, his influence on mainstream entertainment is immense - in the jerky credit sequences and montages, the ubiquitous voice-overs, and the crisscrossing story-lines (**The Log**, **Made in Hong Kong**, **Once upon a Time in Triad Society 2**). Moreover, Wong has deep roots in popular cinema; as Shu Kei points out in his interview here, in the local context Wong's movies are packaged like all the others, with top stars and market-ready soundtracks. Wong seems to have encouraged many local filmmakers to take chances, to retrofit his avant-garde experiments to the demands of more audience-friendly filmmaking. The results, in everything from **The Blade** to **Too Many Ways to Be Number One**, have often proven exhilarating.

One theme of these interviews is that no longer having to make pan-Asian product has given filmmakers the freedom to introduce stronger local flavors. The **Young and Dangerous** cycle, updating the heroic Triad movies, is steeped in the atmosphere of Wanchai, while **Comrades**, **Full Throttle**, **Hu-du-men**, and **Lifeline** quietly assume that probing the niches of local life offers rich rewards. Moreover, these films and others reveal a new interest in careful scripting and subtle acting, while still maintaining the kinetic thrust and unabashed sentiment that make this cinema among the most gripping in film history.

In all, some of Hong Kong's finest films have been made in the last half-dozen years, during the purported collapse of the industry. Hong Kong's business may be dented by Hollywood imports and some of its talent may emigrate. Yet in the hands of Peter Chan, Johnnie To, Andrew Lau, and the other creative people skilfully questioned by Miles Wood, Hong Kong cinema can continue its unique tradition of audacious, unpretentious, and delightful popular moviemaking.

David Bordwell is Professor of Film Studies at the University of Wisconsin, and is one of the world's most respected film historians. He is currently completing a book on Hong Kong cinema.

introduction

Cine-East: Hong Kong Cinema Through the Looking Glass is not the first English language publication on the subject of Hong Kong film, and will certainly not be the last. Indeed, it is hoped this book you are now reading will be only the first in a **Cine-East** series, providing continuing coverage of the ever changing film industry of Hong Kong. The rise in profile of Hong Kong movies during the nineties, initially chiefly due to the success of the films of John Woo in the West, and now, further spurred by Jackie Chan's attempts to "break America", has inevitably led to several "guides" to this most prolific and exciting of national cinemas.

Many factors, however, have led to a great deal of misinformation, and attention has generally focussed on particular areas (e.g. martial arts films), resulting in a misleading and unrepresentative portrait of the sheer wealth and breadth of Hong Kong cinema. **Cine-East** is less a "guide" and more a peek through a few open doors to try and get a better perspective of what the Hong Kong film industry is *really* like, with some help from those who *really* know.

The people interviewed herein were chosen because they have all contributed work that I felt worthy of discussion and because they have not been widely covered in English-language publications, while at the same time I have also tried to present as balanced a picture as possible by featuring filmmakers and performers from different strands and genres. If their words help paint a clearer picture of the process of making and distributing movies in Hong Kong then all well and good; if your interest is piqued to check out their films then even better.

PETER CHAN

In 1997, at the 16th Hong Kong Film Awards, Peter Chan Ho-san's **COMRADES: A LOVE STORY**, a nostalgic tale of two Chinese emigrants whose paths cross over a ten-year span in Hong Kong and New York, took an unprecedented nine prizes, marking a perhaps grudging acceptance of Chan's position as one of Hong Kong's premier directors.

on the set of
Comrades: Almost a Love Story

After working in various capacities in the Hong Kong film industry for several years he helped set up U.F.O. (United Filmmakers Organization) in 1991 and made a string of commercially successful films, including **TOM, DICK & HAIRY** (an humorous but honest exploration of the problems of relationships through the romances of three bachelors who share an apartment) and **HE AIN'T HEAVY, HE'S MY FATHER** (in which a man comes to understand his father after being magically transported back in time to meet him when young), but despite two nominations for best film his movies often received a less-than-kind reception from critics; Tony Rayns, for example, dismissed **HE'S THE WOMAN, SHE'S THE MAN**, a splendid comedy of gender confusion with Leslie Cheung's music producer falling in love with protégé Anita Yuen while believing her to be male, and Chan's biggest hit to date, as "Quintessential phoney Hong Kong sexual liberalism."

Chan may be the region's most Americanised film-maker (his films often reworking themes and ideas from Hollywood movies) so it should perhaps come as no great surprise that a possible link-up with Steven Spielberg is in the pipeline.

Despite having just spoken at a conference debating the current state of Hong Kong Cinema, Chan talked for over an hour and a half in the coffee bar of the Ramada Hotel, about his own films as a director and those he wrote and produced for U.F.O. breaking off only once to sign autographs for some young fans.

陳可辛

Miles Wood:
*I was watching John Woo's **HEROES SHED NO TEARS** recently on tape and there in the end credits was your name.*

Peter Chan Ho-san:
That was my very first movie when I came back to Hong Kong on a summer vacation. It was meant to be a summer job! I was studying film in Los Angeles at the time, but I never graduated. I never went back! I started off as an interpreter but then I became a jack-of-all-trades, third AD, production assistant, almost everything. Then I took care of post-production when the film came back from location in Thailand. After that my first couple of years were pretty good.

You then worked on some Jackie Chan films.

I was doing a lot of big-budget films. That was the heyday of Hong Kong cinema. Every single one of Sammo Hung and Jackie Chan's films were shot abroad so I was in Spain, France and Yugoslavia for two-and-a-half years making three or four movies before I finally set my feet back in Hong Kong again; that was about 1986. I turned to Associate Producing with a film called **SWORN BROTHERS**, then from there I stopped production for a while and joined Eric Tsang, who's like my mentor, and he took me away from Golden Harvest, and I was working as an administrative and distribution executive in his company. That was the worst one year in my life because I had to wear a suit and tie, make deals and talk to people. I decided that's not what I wanted to do, so I quit and started producing independently, because now I had that production experience and the distribution experience. And the first film was called **NEWS ATTACK**.

It's quite a powerful newspaper drama.

It's about three journalists. It's off-beat for Hong Kong standards, but for the West it would seem pretty commercial and mainstream. It's about three reporters who fight the system and try to get the real story out there, and it plays loosely against the world stock market crash of '87, which hit Hong Kong badly because it closed the market for four days. We loosely based it on a tycoon in Hong Kong who tried to hide some facts.
    For the midnight show, it was the time of the Million People March and so we had to march, then go into the cinema to see the takings and come back out and march again. It came out on the weekend of June 4th; on the very day. It was totally forgotten.
    After that came **CURRY AND PEPPER** which was my first commercial success and got me my first directing gig. It gave me bargaining power to do **ALAN AND ERIC**, which was

陳可辛

my first film as a director. **CURRY AND PEPPER** is a very commercial film. It was rather different then in Hong Kong, because it's quite similar to a Hollywood buddy cops movie, with action and comedy, and it was when Chiau Sing-chi was on the way up. He wasn't a big star then.

Alan Tam, Eric Tsang and Maggie Cheung in **Alan and Eric: Between Hello And Goodbye**

ALAN & ERIC: BETWEEN HELLO AND GOODBYE was made a year before you started U.F.O.

I was with Impact. I was pretty lucky. After the failure of **NEWS ATTACK** I got a producing contract with Impact films and they really gave me a lot of freedom, as both a producer and a director. I could almost do whatever I wanted, with a reasonable price tag. You could really experiment with new subject matter because foreign sales were doing so well you could always cover yourself when you were doing it. But unfortunately, that was a time when a lot of bad films were made. People didn't take advantage of the distribution system where they could take the money and make better films. Instead, they took the money and made cheaper films so they could make more money. It's part of the '97 thinking; make the money quick and run mentality.

How was working with Maggie Cheung back then compared to recently on **COMRADES***?*

Not that different. She's very articulate and very intelligent and she also likes to discuss her role in depth when she takes the film seriously, as opposed to most Chinese or Hong Kong

陳可辛

Tony Leung Ka Fai and Tony Leung Chiu Wai in **Tom, Dick and Hairy**

actresses who just come in, do whatever you tell them to, and go, without knowing what the character is about. She's done really commercial, slapstick films where she probably won't even bother talking to the director, but she's a pretty serious actress and a lot of directors would probably think she's asking too many questions, because this is Hong Kong and nobody has the time, but I really enjoyed working with her because she gave a lot of input and really understood the character. The only difference is not in terms of attitude; she's a lot more relaxed now. She's way past the "trying to impress" stage, which makes her even more seasoned and look so much better on screen.

After **ALAN AND ERIC** we made a film I like to call inspired by, but a lot of people call ripped off from, **THE WONDER YEARS**, which is one of my favourite TV series. We thought we'd make the HK version of it; **YESTERYOU, YESTERME, YESTERDAY**.

I must confess when I saw the film I didn't realise it was meant to be a version of **THE WONDER YEARS**.

I produced it with Samson Chui, who directed it, with Impact but it was shelved because it was deemed not commercial enough. They said that nobody wants to see a kids' movie, even though we told them it's really a film about grown-ups. So I was quite disappointed with the industry at that moment, and that's why we formed UFO, and made our first film called **THE DAYS OF BEING DUMB**. It's a parody of all the action films that were being made at the time. We didn't want to make a gangster film

because we didn't know how to do action, so we made a spoof of one... That film did okay, but we were making too few movies in the year, so the company was going through a lot of problems.

Tony Leung Ka Fai and Tony Leung Chiu Wai in **He Ain't Heavy, He's My Father**

Then we made **TOM, DICK & HAIRY**. At first it was shelved, but then it was screened when the market was flooded with sword-fight films, a genre that died instantly, so in early 1993 it scored very good box office. When that did well, they took **YESTERYOU, YESTERME, YESTERDAY**, which had been shelved for two years, and released it as a follow-up hit to **TOM, DICK & HAIRY**! Even though it's a different age group the theme is the same. It's about city folks, sex, and relationships and it did really well.

Then we made **HE AIN'T HEAVY, HE'S MY FATHER**, an idea we got from a couple of high school kids who actually came to the office, about an old man who fell into the fountain of youth and becomes a young man and the father and son become good friends because then their age difference is gone. But I thought no-one would take the fountain of youth seriously so we made it the kid going back in time to see his father in his youth, and then we also realised that by putting him in the past we eliminate the father and son role. Because Chinese believe the problem between father and son is not because of personality but because of their roles. So if we rid them of their roles then they can become equals and all the problems will be gone. And we also took the old fifties and sixties Cantonese films and converted some of the formulas from them that were so tear-jerking and tacky. So it became a comedy and a bittersweet relationship film at the same time.

陳可辛

Leslie Cheung and Carina Lau in **He's The Woman, She's The Man**

That film also did very well, and after that we made **HE'S THE WOMAN, SHE'S THE MAN** and then we started to develop other films on the side like **TWENTYSOMETHING** and a sequel to **YESTERYOU, YESTERME, YESTERDAY** entitled **OVER THE RAINBOW, UNDER THE SKIRT**. So that would be the end of the first wave of UFO films.

The second wave would be **HAPPY HOUR, HEAVEN CAN'T WAIT** and **WHATEVER WILL BE, WILL BE**, and **AGE OF MIRACLES**, which was made in 1994 and should have come out in '95 but actually didn't come out until '96. I think our mentality and the company's attitude towards filmmaking has changed a lot in the past three or four years, both in the way we perceive our own movies and adapt to the market and the system, and our own maturity.

You've used Anita Yuen several times in your films. What do you think is her appeal?

DAYS OF BEING DUMB was her first film and she got a best newcomer award for that. I wasn't really impressed with her then, but I was totally impressed with her in **TOM, DICK & HAIRY**; I thought that was probably her best role to date, because I know how young and inexperienced she was and she was doing something totally beyond her comprehension and she did such a great job. We were very insecure about casting her and we were about to replace her before the first day of shooting because we had a dispute over the fact that we wanted her to wear a bra and she didn't want to wear a bra. I thought if an actress can argue with you about wearing a bra then she

陳
可
辛

Leslie Cheung and Anita Yuen in
He's The Woman, She's The Man

doesn't understand the character, so as I said, we were on the verge of replacing her, until we put her in front of the camera on the first day of shooting and she was like, "Wow!" And that was when I really fell in love with her as an actress. Then I started casting her over and over again. It's not easy working with her because she's a brat; she was spoiled rotten. But we became friends and had a love/hate relationship. And yet, sometimes I can't stand her on set. You know, she just can't control herself. So every time I finish making a movie with her I wish I would never work with again, but every time I do casting, I think of her, because she's good.

She is good, but she seems to take a lot of, shall we say, indifferent roles. Why do you think this is?

Money. She's materialistic, like all of us. All Hong Kong actresses take anything, and the reason she's doing more is that she's more famous, and so she should not feel guilty for taking more roles. Anybody else would take them. There is no "serious actress" in Hong Kong; they can be a serious actress in one movie and a total disaster in another, depending on what the movie is. Even Maggie Cheung did her share of shitty movies. That's the way Hong Kong works: make the money quick and run; because the turnover is so quick and the budget so low, the amount of money you make is very small compared to Hollywood. So this is the way to survive.

One of the greatest actors from Hong Kong, Chow Yun-fat, who everyone revered and admired, taught a lot of young actors that it doesn't matter how many films you do as long as

陳可辛

you do one good one every few films. Because he was doing tons of bad films before he made it; and then as long as you do one good one every year or two, it's okay.

You've been accused of ripping off Hollywood films, such as **VICTOR/VICTORIA** *and* **BACK TO THE FUTURE**...

Which I deny, I know **HE AIN'T HEAVY...** has the premise of **BACK TO THE FUTURE** but I have to be honest I was not pleased with the movie. It's a failed attempt, because I did not pull it through. That was probably the best idea I've ever come up with, the film I most wanted to make, but we - me and my partner Chui, we co-directed it - messed up by being too greedy.
    So I went on to do **AGE OF MIRACLES** which is more or less a remake of **HE AIN'T HEAVY...** It's about mother and son and a miracle that solves the problem between the two generations, but I think I screwed up again. So if I'm given the chance I'll probably do it a third time, some day, maybe as an English-language picture. But I think the only similarity with **BACK TO THE FUTURE** was the premise; going back in time. But anybody can do that.

Are you consciously trying to take stories or ideas that have been used in America and give them a new slant.

In a way, because when I was doing **YESTERYOU, YESTERME, YESTERDAY** I had a strong urge to watch **THE WONDER YEARS** as a movie in Hong Kong. So I made it so I can watch it. It's as simple as that. Part 2 was more original. Part 1 had some gags we actually took from **THE WONDER YEARS**, but about a year after **YESTERYOU, YESTERME, YESTERDAY** was released I saw the last episode, and it just blew me away; after the first two seasons the series hadn't been that interesting. It was a heartbreaker and because of that last monologue, where the family are all together on the 4th July and then Daniel Stern starts telling what happens 2 years later, how his mother became a very independent working woman after his father died. So Part 2 was a totally new creation but with that monologue to end the picture. And that turned out to be my favourite film of those I've done even though I did not direct it. The director Joe Ma went on to de **FEEL 100%**; it's my favourite of his also.

TWENTYSOMETHING *presents a very realistic depiction of sex.*

We did a lot of research on the streets of Lan Kwai Fong. Westerners probably don't see anything wrong with it, or anything strange about it, because this is happening all over the world, the club scene, but a lot of Hong Kong people are not

陳可辛

Twenty Something

exposed to it. There is a small group of young people who are living at night, after work, and I just thought there was a movie to be made showing how they live. I was trying to be objective, not making judgements whether it's right or wrong, although it's not objective enough. I still think one-night stands or club-hopping and having an active sex life is not right or wrong but down to whether your own morality can take it. As expected it became very controversial, and all the critics wrote about it and a lot of radio programs talked about it, and when it was released it made a lot of noise and was quite a successful low-budget film. But I wouldn't say **TWENTYSOMETHING** represents Hong Kong. It's a very extreme example of Hong Kong's young people. Very few people live like that, to be honest. They think that other people are like that but other people think *they* are like that. The club scene is relatively small. Everywhere in the world there is a club scene; it's just a little smaller here. I think the best achievement was the way that Teddy Chan - who's third feature film this was - directed the new actors.

Actually Teddy Chan was directing a film *[DOWNTOWN TORPEDOES]* in which a prop man died in an explosion just yesterday, and that's never happened before in Hong Kong. Because the Hong Kong Government never gave permission to use explosives in filmmaking. But it's so ridiculous because they know it's going on. Now it's a big issue, and they will try to prosecute the film company. It's regrettable that it's taken somebody's life to get people to sit down and talk.

*Can you talk about **AGE OF MIRACLES** and the question of Anita Yuen's make-up, which got a lot of attention?*

Anita Yuen (left) in old-age make-up in **Age Of Miracles**

陳
可
辛

It's a big hindrance; it's the biggest stumbling block I have met. I still don't know today if I had cast a new actress in that role if the film would have done better, because a lot of people like that film but they don't like the make-up and they don't like Anita Yuen doing it.

But I sort-of had no choice. I was in America talking with Tsui Chin, who was in **JOY LUCK CLUB** as Tamlyn Tomita's mother, and we toyed with the idea of her playing the role. But I could not have cast her, because the film is not only about old age. There is this young version of the same woman and throughout the film we have to see a woman with all the responsibility of the family, and show how Chinese women age, so I wanted to cast one actress to play both roles. And I was too confident after doing **HE AIN'T HEAVY...** I had old age make-up on Tony Leung and Carina Lau and that went very, very well. I thought they, especially Tony Leung, looked very believable and I thought I could get away with it. And I went back to the same effects house and spent a fortune to fly in the special effects person from Hollywood. Actually a very funny episode of the story is that he was nominated, and won, the award for **BRAM STOKER'S DRACULA**, and he was nominated again this year for James Woods' make-up for **GHOSTS OF MISSISSIPPI**. And when I went to see **GHOSTS OF MISSISSIPPI** last spring he looked exactly like Tony Leung in **HE AIN'T HEAVY...**! I said, "Tony Leung wore that make-up four years ago!" You know, Tony Leung looked like a "gwailo" - he doesn't look very Chinese - because he doesn't know Chinese features so he has to use very Western features when applying the make-up. Anyway, so I went to LA and hired him to come to Hong Kong for three months to do the make-up and I was shooting over-schedule and over-budget; I originally thought we'd finish in a month-and-a-half. But it didn't look good. It was summer and it was hot. We were shooting on a sound-stage with no air-conditioning and it took Anita Yuen three hours to put that make-up on every day, and then when she's working, after half-an-hour she started to sweat between the prosthetic and her face, and she was going through that every day. And it was tough on her. It affected her performance. So looking back maybe I did the wrong thing. But what's done is done.

It featured a recurring image in your work, the Statue of Liberty.

The Statue of Liberty is something I like very much. For **AGE OF MIRACLES** we took the Statue and put it in the middle of Nathan Road, with snow and everything! It was one of the magic-realism fantasy sequences. And I've been criticised a lot about it; they brand me too Americanised; this Chinese who loves America. I don't love America but I grew up reading about it and I've always been touched by films of immigrants moving to America. It's not what America stands for, but it's my perception of America. I thought the Statue of Liberty the easiest, most convenient, and effective device to use in that particular scene. Even the first movie I made had a glimpse of the Statue.

*UFO's next film **HAPPY HOUR** was directed by Benny Chan*

I saw **BIG BULLET** just last week and was blown away. It's a great experience working with Benny because he's so independent. His sense of timing, his editing in the movie is so strong, so well synchronised. He is very, very local; from the grass roots. He has a perspective that I don't have because I grew up elsewhere and I've been travelling.

It's a project that he set up. He worked on the script and he was trying to sell it to another company, to Johnnie To, in fact, but he didn't buy it. And one day I was talking to the writer who was working on another film for me and she mentioned it to me, and I said I loved it, it was a great idea, and let's do it. So I called Benny, who I'd never met, and we started talking and we did it. But it's Benny and Susan's baby.

It deals with quite a controversial issue - three friends find themselves arrested for the rape of a woman they picked up in a club. Was it successful in Hong Kong?

Mediocre. It's probably the first UFO film that did not do 10 million. It's the beginning of a streak of bad luck for UFO, to be very Chinese. Because the next year we had problems with **HEAVEN CAN'T WAIT** and **AGE OF MIRACLES**. And then people started saying the magic is gone.

So like I said there are three stages of UFO. It all started with **HE AIN'T HEAVY, HE'S MY FATHER** and **TOM DICK AND HAIRY** when we were very certain of our ability to make a commercial movie for the market.

Then we hit '94 with **HE'S THE WOMAN, SHE'S THE MAN**, **OVER THE RAINBOW**, **UNDER THE SKIRT** and a ghost movie, **THE RETURNING**. It's an eleven-year-old story that I had, which derived from my childhood experience. It's a real life character; my father was an editor and the character is a legendary writer who used to work with him but whom my father had never met. I was going to produce and Chi Lee would direct it as a film for UFO in 1992, but because of Leslie Cheung bowing out we never had the right actor to do it. So we shelved it until '94 when Jacob Cheung took it from the shelf and said he could do his take on it. So that was a very good year for UFO, and after that we made some money, bought our own office, and then became very ambitious and I made the over-budget, over-scheduled **AGE OF MIRACLES** and then it was like the second wave of a streak of bad luck; films did not really perform. So we sat down and evaluated our strengths and weaknesses and then we started to do some movies that we had wanted to do. That's the third stage, with **LOST AND FOUND** and **COMRADES**. And it's a slight departure from the way we made movies: it's not as calculated and we don't really take the market into as much consideration as we had, but only because the films are cheap. It's not because we've changed or anything, but we can afford to when we make a HK$20/30m picture.

COMRADES and WHO'S THE MAN, WHO'S THE WOMAN were shot at the same time?

Together. To tell that story you have to go back to the success of **HE'S THE WOMAN, SHE'S THE MAN**. That put a lot of pressure on my shoulders as a filmmaker. I know that it's not right, but after a hit you're very limited, because you have to make another hit. Especially when you run the company! Shu Kei's right, we're not independent in the true sense; we're just a company that's called "independent" but it's not the "indie spirit." Anyway, after that I could almost do what I wanted to do. I had the leverage. I chose **AGE OF MIRACLES** because it's something I really wanted to do. **HE'S THE WOMAN, SHE'S THE MAN**, including script, only took me about four to five months. The shooting was only about seven weeks including post-production. **AGE OF MIRACLES** took eighteen months! So I put all my time and effort into that movie and it did not come out too well, so in those two years we lost a lot of money and we had to get ourselves a deal in the studio. We had left the studio in the first place to form UFO because we wanted autonomy and now - because number one, the market is going down - getting back to the studio is to our advantage.

陳
可
辛

Leslie Cheung, Eric Tsang and Anita Yuen in **Who's The Woman, Who's The Man**

Being in a lot of debt was not so bad after all, because UFO could not have survived on our own. We were barely covering our costs, and now we had more leverage because we had proved ourselves to be commercially viable. So they would not really mess with us. So now our relationship with Golden Harvest is pretty much that with the right price tag we could probably do what we want, so we decided to talk to Golden Harvest and the first thing they want, the very basis of the agreement, is I have to make a sequel to **HE'S THE WOMAN, SHE'S THE MAN**, which I'd never thought of doing at all.

When I knew that, then I fought and wrestled with the idea for about a month and came up with something that I always wanted to make about relationships. There are films that I really like, such as **TWO FOR THE ROAD**, which is my favourite movie, and even **INDECENT PROPOSAL** which is also about the uncertainty of relationships. So I wanted to make a film about that issue, about how uncertain relationships are in the nineties, how love is not so dependable or invincible, and I thought of this as a good arena to make that film, using the relationship of Leslie and Anita. You have one movie to establish them as a couple and then what you need to do is break them apart. If Part 1 is a fairy tale, Part 2 is the reality. Even though that's not really commercial, who cares, because I told them this is Part 2 and so nobody messes with my script or even knows what it's about. The problem with Part 2 is, doing a serious movie as a sequel to a very light-hearted, broad comedy is very tough, because as serious as the theme is, you still have to add a list of the other comic ingredients. So it became a bit middle-of-the-road. Neither here nor there. That was probably two or three of my most miserable months when I was doing that

陳可辛

Leon Lai and
Maggie Cheung in
Comrades: Almost a
Love Story

movie. I finished that film in five weeks, intentionally, because I postponed the shoot until the very last minute - five-and-a-half weeks before delivery date - so it was completed, production and post-production, in five-and-a-half weeks. I intentionally did that because I didn't even want to have to think twice after having started making the movie. I just want to finish it in one go. So I told all my crew, my team, that from that day onward, when we start shooting, we probably cannot go home because we won't be able to sleep. We won't be able to rest. That's the bad side. But the good side of it is in five weeks, it's all over.

But when I was making the deal with Golden Harvest, I told them, if you insist I do this I would want to do a small picture on the side that you would otherwise not finance, and that's **COMRADES**. It's the kind of film I could probably not get green-lighted had I not had this picture.

Even with that cast?

Well maybe. But it would be very difficult. So I did both films together. Even now the film is very successful in Hong Kong, South-East Asia, Japan, and Korea but still it's barely breaking even. With copyright, video rights sold and everything, at the end of the day it will probably make less than HK$1 million. So if the film had been less than a phenomenal success it would have lost a lot of money, because of that cast. Because the cast took up half of the budget! So what happens is, I slip that film on the side. I have to shoot the two films together because of

*Cheung Chi Lam,
Jordan Chan and
Andy Hui in
Happy Hour*

scheduling problems and also because after they see the first film they might not let me do the second one.

But I heard a very interesting observation from a friend who is very anti-Communist, and he was very pissed with some of the dialogue at the end of **COMRADES**, where Maggie as a tour guide is talking to some of the mainlanders that want to buy Gucci handbags or whatever and they talk about Hong Kong people moving to China to make money and that it's the place to be, not here; this is the decay of Western civilization. It's the Pacific Rim theory or something... And Maggie smiles and says she's not been back in ten years but is going back the next month; it's like come full circle. I never thought people would take that as a compliment to China, but some of my anti-Communist friends said that's not a good statement to make in the movie.

I thought it was just pathetic for someone to go out for ten years and life has never changed. Ironically the better life is in China, but if she goes back will it be any better? My statement is that it's pathetic that the Chinese have to go from place to place, but anyway my friends who were angry felt good afterwards, because I have Maggie looking up at the Statue of Liberty, and their interpretation of that was that no matter how good China is, there is no liberty or freedom or democracy. But that was not intended. She looked at the Statue because the next shot I was cutting to Leon [Lai] looking at the Statue and I had to have them looking at the same time. I would say it's not intended to be a political film, but all films have some politics in them.

*Jordan Chan,
Ha Ping and Tony
Leung Chiu Wau in*
Heaven Can't Wait

Something that seems inherent in Hong Kong culture, that the film plays with a lot, is the notion of fate.

Endlessly. That's the whole theme of the movie. The beginning of the ending. I guess we need to believe in fate because our lives are so uncertain; our destiny has always been uncertain. It's not about Hong Kongese but about Chinese. For four-hundred years we've been moving around, but the problem with Chinese is wherever they go, they try to go back. When they have a better life they try to go back home, and that is what this film is really about: the way my father's generation... He's second generation Chinese, Thai Chinese; his father and my mother's father went to Thailand as a result of China being poor. A lot of Chinese move to different parts of South East Asia to have a better life. When they do make money they want to send their kids back home because they keep teaching them that they're not Chinese. They have to go to China to find their own identity, then they realise that they're not really Chinese, but it's too late. The lucky ones left before the Cultural Revolution; the least fortunate ones left in the seventies and eighties, and all of them came to Hong Kong because this is the first stop from China. And most of them ended up staying and giving birth to hundreds of thousands of kids like myself. And so Hong Kong is made up of one-third or one-quarter who are descendants of overseas Chinese and 90% if not 100% are people migrating from China.

So fate is important for all Chinese people because just when we thought the best period in Hong Kong is from the late sixties to the early eighties, when it grew as a city, the future is confirmed, and Communism is not going to tamper with Hong Kong, then in 1983 the '97 issue came, and it's another big blow. So it's something that Chinese and Hong Kong people really need. They have to believe that there's someone up there doing all the planning for them, and that it's not just yourself otherwise it would be too much to handle.

*I like **COMRADES** but Hong Kong critics appear to look on it as a major step forward for you and UFO, which would seem to be denigrating your other films, maybe because they're comedies.*

It's because they're commercial. I think there's a problem there. I don't know if it will make them feel any better, but as commercial as they seem they're not making any money. But to me what actually reflects my personality, the way I make movies... I hate to be branded by people and I've been branded that **COMRADES** is what I really wanted to make for a long time and it's something that I could not make and I've been forced to make other films and be calculated and all that. But that's not true. Every single film I'm proud of. Every one was my baby. **COMRADES** is not any more so. To be very honest, it's probably less so than my other films, because **WHO'S THE MAN, WHO'S THE WOMAN** may be a failed attempt, **AGE OF MIRACLES** may be a failed attempt, **HE AIN'T HEAVY, HE'S MY FATHER** may be a failed attempt, but these three films probably deal with something I really want to talk about. They thought I was making these films for the market but actually I was making them for myself.

Critics just can't take comedies seriously.

All over the world.

What I'm attracted to in Hong Kong cinema, and David Bordwell said this very well, is that in many ways it's like the American mainstream cinema of yesteryear, where directors, such as John Ford and Howard Hawks, are trying to do their best, often making personal films in a commercial system.

And whatever would happen to John Ford and Howard Hawks nowadays? Critics love movies, and there are movies that make money; but they never cross. I would love to know if Ford and Hawks were praised in their times. We're looking at them in retrospect.

What lies in the future for Peter Chan and UFO?

UFO is taking a very different route now. We're doing some smaller pictures with the second generation of UFO filmmakers:

陳
可
辛

Takeshi Kaneshiro,
Kelly Chan and Jordan
Chan (with baby) in
Lost and Found

James Yuen, who's been writing scripts for us will do his own production, directing. Chi is doing some films with Media Asia. Jacob is still with UFO. We've made two movies in the last four or five months, one by Jacob *[INTIMATES]*, one by James *[THE WEDDING DAYS]*. I'm taking a year off. I left in December '96 and won't be back until the end of the year and I live now in LA (I live here too!) and I have a project I really want to do in Thailand, that I'm talking to Korean and Japanese investors about.

I'll use my crew in Hong Kong, and I'll use some Hong Kong actors, and some Taiwanese actors. My agents are trying to set up deals so I can get finance in America, but they wanted the film to be in English. They say "**SCHINDLER'S LIST** shouldn't be in English, it should be in German or Yiddish, but if that can be in English why can't your film?" It's a film that takes the theme of **COMRADES** one step further; it's actually the story of my mother and father's generation: second generation Chinese.

The film starts in 1945 after the war. It's very romanticised: under the coconut tree with a bunch of Chinese kids aged about eleven or twelve growing up believing they're Chinese but actually they're Thai. They're not used to cold weather, and they eat hot spicy food, but they have to go back to China to find their identity. And they join the wave of immigrants going to China in the early fifties because of the Chinese take-over in 1959, after which there were a lot of hopes for a new country, a new China. So shiploads of educated intellectuals and students went back

陳
可
辛

*Wu Chien Lien and Tony Leung Chiu Wai in **The Returning***

to China to prove they're Chinese and it was disastrous, because they're discriminated against and a lot fought in the Korean war, and lost their innocence. But I'm trying to make it light! It's heavy enough as a background so I don't want to push a heavy issue. It's about these kids growing up and how they finally got round to leave China and came to Hong Kong, marry, have kids, and not be able to go back because they're blacklisted in Thailand by communists. And some smuggle their way back in with false passports and a lot are left homeless because most that left are privileged people; the poor people could not have left. It was like Hong Kong people going to the West for education. I will use the forties and fifties and maybe the nineties when they're old, but I'll probably skip the Chinese part, not only because it's sensitive politically but also because there's too many films made about the cultural revolution. It becomes a cliché. I will also make some episodes on the Korean War; the Chinese fighting a war that is not their war. And the overseas Chinese are even worse, as they're not even Chinese. So that's hopefully my next project.

You seem to be delving into the nature of being Chinese or Hong Kongese. So what is a Hong Kong person?

Hong Kongese is very apolitical, because as opposed to most Chinese in China, we never had any political oppression. So we don't have that anger, it's not in our system because we never

陳
可
辛

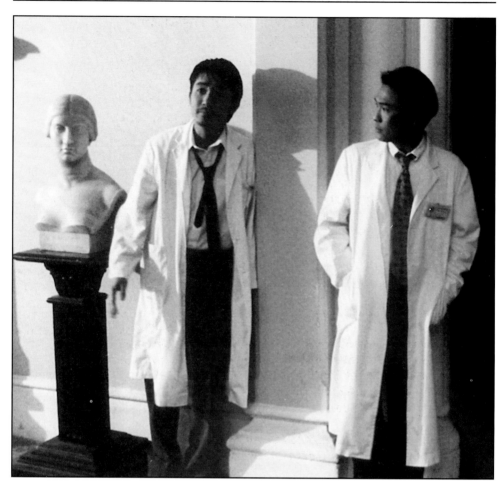

Alex To and Tony Leung Chiu Wai in **Dr. Mack**

had to deal with any political problems. Ask me why Hong Kong films are so apolitical, so commercial. Well, it's because we don't have that thing in us. So we won't have that problem after the take-over because we don't make political films anyway, so to a certain extent we should not be too worried about the Chinese censorship system. But after 1997 we are going to be with China so we might have political oppression, so maybe five or ten years down the line we might have it in us to make films that are political, but right now, we don't have it in our blood. So Hong Kong is changing rapidly. But at the moment it is apolitical, money-driven and ever-changing.

A lot of people will tell you different, but deep down they don't relate to many things that are Chinese. Racially they're Chinese but without any loyalty to any country or Government or authority. But ironically, in some issues they are; such as June 4th where there were more people on the streets than anywhere in the world, and the flood in '91 where Hong Kong probably donated more money than the whole world combined. It's the same complex about the Thai-Chinese wanting to go back; wanting to prove they're Chinese. They want to be something.

You talked of the Chinese overseas. What about the recent work of Hong Kong film-makers in Hollywood?

A film made in Hong Kong with Hong Kong actors will make a lot of money but John Woo's film with Van Damme is a Van Damme film and Hong Kong never really regard their export as a hero; something a little better than traitors, but something not highly respected. Not like Finland with Renny Harlin.

Some people might think that the director will help them; agents may say to the studios that by hiring this director they will have extra X amount of money from the Asian market but I think that's bullshit. Actor maybe, say, Chow Yun-fat. They quote them how much their films made in Hong Kong and they will justify their paycheck, but in reality...

How important are the overseas markets to Hong Kong films now?

Action is good overseas, in Korea, but does not sell in Hong Kong. Taiwan is over and done with. It used to be our biggest market but now zero. Singapore and Malaysia is similar to Hong Kong. Bangkok doesn't buy Hong Kong movies anymore. Video has killed the North American Chinatown theatrical market. So we're talking about US$20 or 30 thousand per blockbuster picture so we don't even take that into consideration.

Compared to Hollywood the distribution networks in Hong Kong are very poorly organised. There are no integrated media conglomerates.

Maybe because the film business has never been seen as completely legitimate in the eyes of business people. At least until the last five years. It was regarded as unprofessional, with Triad involvement, something you don't want to touch. And by the mid-eighties all the studios were gone. There was no long term planning. Just a bunch of fortune hunters out to make a quick buck and run; a lot of small companies, one-third of which were Triad related. It's becoming different, with Hong Kong film being seen as more important, and more and more mediums, such as cable, satellite; so people are buying up film libraries and film rights but it takes time.

Even though Golden Harvest sold many titles to Media Asia two years ago they still have an enormous library, so they will probably still be the strongest company.

We had a mini Hollywood, our own film awards, with even more freedom but when you're not doing well you have to change.

Japanese advertising for *He Ain't Heavy, He's My Father*

*Leon Lai and
Maggie Cheung in*
**Comrades: Almost A
Love Story**

Filmography:

NEWS ATTACK (1989)
CURRY AND PEPPER (1990)
ALAN AND ERIC: BETWEEN HELLO AND GOODBYE
(1991) *[dir]*
DAYS OF BEING DUMB (1992)
TOM, DICK AND HAIRY (1993) *[dir]*
ALWAYS ON MY MIND (1993)
HE AIN'T HEAVY, HE'S MY FATHER (1993)
[co-dir. with Lee Chi Ngai]
TWENTYSOMETHING (1994)
THE RETURNING (1994)
HE'S THE WOMAN, SHE'S THE MAN (1994) *[dir]*
OVER THE RAINBOW, UNDER THE SKIRT (1994)
HAPPY HOUR (1995)
HEAVEN CAN'T WAIT (1995)
WHATEVER WILL BE WILL BE (1995)
THE AGE OF MIRACLES (1996) *[dir]*
THOSE WERE THE DAYS (1996)
WHO'S THE WOMAN, WHO'S THE MAN (1996) *[dir]*
LOST AND FOUND (1996)
COMRADES; ALMOST A LOVE STORY (1996) *[dir]*

陳
可
辛

ПΛGGIE CHEUNG

in The Heroic Trio

張曼玉

Maggie Cheung Man-yuk was born in Hong Kong, but at the age of eight she emigrated to England. On her return to Hong Kong she became a model and competed in the 1983 Miss World, which led to contracts with TVB and Shaw Brothers.

Most people initially noticed her in her first outing in the recurring role of Jackie Chan's beleaguered girlfriend in **POLICE STORY**, while her acting skills steadily matured as she worked with many of Hong Kong's finest film-makers, including Wong Kar-wai (in his brilliant debut **AS TEARS GO BY**, a vivid painting of the "Mean Streets" of Mongkok, and in the internationally acclaimed drama **DAYS OF BEING WILD**), Clara Law (playing a Chinese illegal immigrant facing the harsh realities of life in New York in the truly frightening **FAREWELL CHINA**) and Ann Hui (playing the Hui character herself in the director's semi-autobiographical account of her relationship with her mother **SONG OF THE EXILE**). She was voted best actress in Berlin and Taiwan for her performance as the famous but tragic Chinese movie star Ruan Ling Yu in Stanley Kwan's **CENTRE STAGE** (aka **ACTRESS**) confirming her status as a major star.

In 1994 she retired for two years returning to play alongside Vivian Wu and Michelle Yeoh in Mable Cheung's long-awaited but ultimately disappointing story of **THE SOONG SISTERS**. She embraced the challenge of her first Western role in Olive Assayas's witty, low-budget arthouse success **IRMA VEP** and for Peter Chan's **COMRADES** won the Best Actress Award in the 21st Hong Kong Film Awards.

Maggie Cheung was interviewed at the ICA, when she was in England to attend the 1996 London Film Festival's screening of **IRMA VEP**.

Miles Wood:
Are there any of your early films which you particularly like?

Maggie Cheung Man-yuk:
I'm not ashamed of them but I don't think they're good enough to represent me as an actress because I wasn't an actress at the time. I just did films and I had no idea what I was doing really, so I can't say those films were my work. I think the first one that I could recognise myself as an actress in was **AS TEARS GO BY**, and since there have been four or five award-winning films; but even **DAYS OF BEING WILD**, I don't think I could put it in as my retrospective because I'm not the main lead. It's not *my* film. So I've only really done **ACTRESS** that's *my* film. And the recent one *[COMRADES: ALMOST A LOVE STORY]* I kind-of like but I'm not sure if the Western audience would like it because it's very... it's a story about people from China wanting to go to Hong Kong. So it's a very Hong Kong people's film. You have to understand the situation how people from Hong Kong see people from China and why they want to go to Hong Kong. It's very local. It's showing right now and it's doing really well and it has very nice moments in it. It's very sensitive about how we feel.

top:
with Alan Tam in
Alan and Eric: Between
Hello and Goodbye

above:
in Actress

with Jackie Chan in
Police Story

The first change in my career was **AS TEARS GO BY**, and then actually **FULL MOON IN NEW YORK** got me my first award which really meant something to me, though I don't love the film that much. Then **DAYS OF BEING WILD**, although the film is the star; Wong Kar Wai is the star, not the actors from it. I've heard millions of people say they loved the film but they didn't say they loved me. But it's left a good mark on my career. People will talk about it and it's something they will recognise me for apart from the action films. And there are a bunch of cinema-goers who love Asian films, but just action films, and they will talk about the **POLICE STORY**'s and the **HEROIC TRIO**'s but there's another side of the audience who love **DAYS OF BEING WILD** and **ACTRESS**.

ACTRESS was the first serious recognition I got as a serious actress.

Just in Hong Kong or internationally?

with Brigitte Lin in
Red Dust

Internationally because of the Berlin Award. It was big news in Hong Kong, in that they were happy for me and also that a Chinese actress got recognised. It's the first part I had when I was the lead from the first scene until the last. In **DAYS OF BEING WILD** I just didn't have much to do.

*So was **ACTRESS** the first film you did much research for?*

Yes. Stanley Kwan was doing research two years before the film started. So he had this pile of information and tapes and we were in Shanghai for four months and the first two were just getting into the part so it was very rare for Hong Kong - I felt that to do that part properly and well, I must know it well. I would even fall asleep thinking about her. She really haunted me for those four months. Many people would say they hated it, but of course, you can't please everybody. I was very different from in my other films.

RED DUST *was excellent but you were kind of overshadowed by Brigitte Lin.*

Well she's the lead. It was a favour.

*You worked with Wong Kar-wai a third time in **ASHES OF TIME** but your part is quite small.*

I don't even know my own name in the film! A lot of people tell me they love me in that film and I'll ask them "Who did I play?" and they'll say something that I didn't play, and I say "No, you got wrong. You didn't recognise me really!"

張曼玉

Poster for
The Soong Sisters

It's not really recognising my face but sorting out who is a really big thing from that film because it's very confusing. The first time I saw it I thought "What's it about?" But the second time I thought, "actually it's quite good," and then the third time I really loved it, when I actually understood the meaning of the film. I think it's a great meaning, and I haven't really seen a film with that message and you know it's so true: you just have one moment in your life and it's gone forever. It's very touching for me.

Does it help to know the book to understand it?

It's easier because I recognise the characters but I still couldn't figure out what they were trying to do and what they were trying to say. There's just so many dialogues all at once and you really have to listen and feel what they're saying. I suppose it's *less* confusing for Chinese people.

There is a noticeable gap in your filmography.

After '93/94 I stopped working for a couple of years and I picked up again in Spring '95. I did **SOONG SISTERS** and that was about four months in China (April to August) and then I took a rest - there was nothing interesting around - until Olivier's project came around, and I did that in January '96 and that was done by February, and in March I did another film **[COMRADES]**. I've done three films since I started working again.

*In **IRMA VEP**, how close is the part to yourself?*

Close to... It's me! But not completely, because I have more to me than ninety minutes; there's more than has been exposed on screen. But in general the way I reacted to the people and the dialogues which I would add myself, were really quite me.

張曼玉

Was much of the dialogue improvised?

Yes. Olivier wanted me to add more stuff from myself. He didn't know me that well at the time. Now he knows me better because since then we've spent some time together, but when he wrote the script he just had a vague image of who I am. So, when I stepped on set he said basically, "Maggie, be yourself." If I wasn't comfortable with the line he wrote I would just say something that I would say, but more or less to the same meaning because we have to stick to the situations. You can't just go off from the story. So I improvised a lot. The most I have done in all my films. And the way I played it, I tried not to think about how I'm going to play it at all, just came very naturally. It's like an interview. I don't plan what I'm going to tell you, I just have to react to what you ask me. So that was the attitude I had to play the part.

top:
*in **Green Snake***

above:
*in **Irma Vep***

top:
Executioners

above:
*Japanese Advertising for **Full Moon in New York***

*So was **IRMA VEP** a deliberate decision to work outside Hong Kong?*

I wanted to spend time in Paris, yes, and to get to know it better. It wasn't ambitious in that it was my first chance to step into the West. Because when I received the script and heard from Olivier how it was going to be made it was going to be very low budget. A small little film; just intimate. How I pictured it at the time was it would probably show in one of the art theatres in Paris and it's not going to travel any more than that, and probably no-one would ever find out that I made it. I didn't even tell people in Hong Kong I was making it until after it's finished, and they found out and I admitted it. I flew to Cannes and it got some kind of attention. It travelled much further than I imagined. Actually, now it's going to show in all the cities in the world. In the States, London, Europe, and in Taiwan, Hong Kong, Singapore, Korea. So I'm glad I wasn't *too* lazy on that film, thinking I can get away with it because no-one's going to see it. I did try my best!

You have mentioned in the past about your film-making ambitions.

French poster for
Irma Vep

The way I want to make my own film... I don't think there's a film in Hong Kong that resembles it. It would be quite personal. We'll see. I'm not in a hurry to do that because I'm quite scared of doing it. It's easy to say "I have this dream, I want to do it." I don't really care if it stays like a dream forever. It's nice to have that

SONG OF THE EXILE

墨天のロンドン 逆光のマカオ
雨の香港──秋風の九州湯布院
異郷をさすらうふたりの女
──娘と母 ふたりの女
その愛の苦悩、望郷の涙に浮き彫る
静かな"アジアの慟哭"

90年アジア太平洋映画祭グランプリ 90年リミニ(伊)映画祭グランプリ
90年台湾・中時晩報電影奬最優秀作品賞 90年金馬奬最優秀脚本賞
監督:許鞍華アン・ホイ
脚本:呉念真ウー・ニェンチェン/製作:廖慶平ジェレンタ・リウ
製作総指揮:綜念鎮モン・フー、王羽ジミー・ウォング、趙琦彬ベニー・チャオ
撮影:鍾志文デビド・チョン/美術:柔仲文イー・チョムマン/音楽:陳陽チェン・ヤン
発行人:林聖飛リン・ドンフェイ、周乃忠チョウ・ナイチュン

陸小芬ルー・シャオフェン、張曼玉マギー・チャン
李子雄レイ・ナーホン 田豊ティエン・ファン 加地健太郎 逸見慶子
1990年/香港・台湾合作/カラー
配給:ヘラルド・エース、日本ヘラルド映画

Song of the Exile

dream and not make it happen, because once it happens it might be a nightmare and it would not be as beautiful as I imagine it to be, and then there would be other problems. Let it stay that way until I'm really ready for it, or I feel it's time to do.

You seem to know your limitations. For instance, you've not gone into singing.

I don't believe in that. I'm not saying I'm a good singer or a bad singer, but I don't believe if you want to be taken seriously, and see yourself as a professional actress, that you should start singing. I can't spread myself in so many ways as some artists can.

*You're perceived differently in the West compared to the way you're perceived in Hong Kong, because here people tend to know you from the likes of **THE HEROIC TRIO**.*

I'm aware that there are fans who are crazy about Hong Kong films but I'm not aware that there are people who are crazy about Maggie Cheung. So I never really met anyone who said "I watch all the Hong Kong films because of you." I don't see I have any real fans, but it doesn't matter, you know, as long as they keep on watching Hong Kong films and keep up to date with what they're doing there.

*top:
in The Soong Sisters*

*above:
in Actress*

Poster for
Dragon Inn

張
曼
玉

What do you think of the current situation?

Only good films survive at the box office.

Good in terms of what?

Good in terms of it has to be new and creative, serious, sincere; and I think the audiences are much more fussy than they were, so you have to have something to attract them and it has to be good.

*The **YOUNG AND DANGEROUS** films have been enormously successful.*

Yes, they were the 'noise' this year. The director was the cameraman who did **AS TEARS GO BY**, so to me it's still Wong Kar-wai who dominates.

Do you trust Hong Kong critics?

Only a few. Some of them "get paid"! They buy them dinner or they have a good relationship with the director or company. But it's the same everywhere else.

Do you still subscribe to the idea of oscillating between art and commercial films.

Yes. Actually, I don't choose from what they are. I choose projects with the people, scripts, the combination of things. And

above:
in Green Snake

below left:
publicity still for
The Soong Sisters

I really don't care if it's a comedy or what, you know. I can still have a good trip on that film. That's how I see it. Each film is a trip for me.

How much is it for the audience? With the star system in Hong Kong you seem very close to them.

Yes, but I'm kinda falling out with that. I'm very much into doing what I enjoy more than calculating, "Is this going to bring my career to a higher level?", because you just can't please them. And I believe eventually if I just stick to my principles they will appreciate me in some way or other.

So if other projects were to arise in the West?

There are projects that have come my way since **IRMA VEP** but I'm not sure about them. There's one really strange one that I would like to do, that I'm afraid to do, but I can't tell you. It will

affect me personally and my career. It will affect my career maybe in a nice way, but it will affect me in a bad way personally. I don't think I can stand to be bad.

張曼玉

in Actress

Selected Filmography

PRINCESS CHARMING (1984)
POLICE STORY (1985)
THE SEVENTH CURSE (1986)
HEARTBEAT 100 (1987)
AS TEARS GO BY (1988)
THE BACHELOR'S SWAN SONG (1989)
A FISHY STORY (1989)
HEARTS NO FLOWERS (1989)
ICEMAN COMETH (1989)
HEARTS INTO HEARTS (1990)
FULL MOON IN NEW YORK (1990)
SONG OF THE EXILE (1990)
THE DRAGON FROM RUSSIA (1990)
RED DUST (1990)
FAREWELL CHINA (1990)
DAYS OF BEING WILD (1990)
ALAN AND ERIC: BETWEEN HELLO AND GOODBYE (1991)
ALL'S WELL, ENDS WELL (1992)
ACTRESS / CENTRE STAGE (1992)
DRAGON INN (1992)
MOON WARRIORS (1992)
THE HEROIC TRIO (1993)
THE FIRST SHOT (1993)
ENIGMA OF LOVE (1993)
THE MAD MONK (1993)
GREEN SNAKE (1993)
EXECUTIONERS (1993)
THE BAREFOOT KID (1993)
FLYING DAGGER (1993)
THE NEW AGE OF LIVING TOGETHER / IN-BETWEEN (1994)

張曼玉

ASHES OF TIME (1994)
COMRADES: ALMOST A LOVE STORY (1996)
IRMA VEP (1996)
THE SOONG SISTERS (1997)

Poster for
Enigma of Love

Lau ching wan

in Expect The Unexpected

劉青雲

Dubbed by noted film historian David Bordwell as Hong Kong's answer to Spencer Tracy, Lau Ching-wan has earned growing respect from viewers, critics and his fellow professionals alike. After spending years in television his big break in movies came in 1993 when he starred alongside Anita Yuen in Derek Yee's hugely successful tear-jerking romance *C'EST LA VIE, MON CHERIE*. In that year's Hong Kong Film Awards, he was nominated twice, for *C'EST LA VIE...* (which scooped the six other major awards!) and for Wellson Chin's chilling *THOU SHALT NOT SWEAR* (the first in a series of horror films that use a date for their Chinese title), and was nominated again in 1997 for Benny Chan's rousing actioner *BIG BULLET* and in 1998 for Ringo Lam's *FULL ALERT*. However, he has yet to win!

He now has a long list of film credits to his name, appearing in both leading and supporting roles, ranging from romantic dramas (which often re-teamed him with Anita Yuen) to comedies (such as the hilarious 1995 farce *TRICKY BUSINESS*, which cruelly lampooned *C'EST LA VIE...*) to thrillers (his part in Ringo Lam's *FULL ALERT*), his presence often adding depth to otherwise lightweight productions. Most recently he has starred in a series of films - as the hardened veteran Fire Chief in Johnnie To's 1997 fire-fighting drama *LIFELINE*; as a priest accused of rape in Derek Chiu's *FINAL JUSTICE* (also 1997); as a tattooed shaven-headed hitman in Patrick Yau's *THE LONGEST NITE* (1998) - all produced by Milkyway Image, in whose office we spent over an hour chatting.

Miles Wood:
How did you start out?

Lau Ching-wan:
It's a long story. When I was seventeen years old I saw a television advert for the TVB training school. But it was not my idea to go: it was my father's idea. When he saw it, he said "if you've got nothing to do why don't you try it?"

So you didn't want to be an actor?

My first dream was that I wanted to be a spaceman, but I knew this was impossible. Anyway, I passed an exam, a screen test, and went to the school. But in that year, 1983, what they needed was some handsome guy, you know. I'm different from all the other guys; so many students look at me and think "why does that guy come to this place?" I don't even look like a Chinese! But by the time I finished the training school I felt I had to be an actor and after a couple of more years I felt I was an actor. It's a very interesting job. So, for over ten years I was acting in television series. I enjoyed it. Now I'm thirty-three years old. For ten years my working hours were 6am-2am. It took all my time. I gave up many things, my girlfriend, everything, for this job. But I never know what my future will be. Noone can know that they will be a star. I just do it. From twenty-one to twenty-nine, was just lost. I was living in another world. But I really enjoy acting, because I have the chance to play so many different roles: doctor, soldier, anything. It's amazing, because when you play a role it's not real, yet it is real. So you can love a girl but not have any responsibilities! Better than real life!

Did you have any choice in the roles you took?

No. You could choose to do it or not to do it!

So how did you make the transformation from television to film?

I was very lucky. After ten years, I hadn't done anything very special, but I think maybe I had a chance to leave. I was getting old. When a man is about twenty-eight years old he gets nervous. So I really wanted to leave and make movies, because movies make more money; working in TVB you never believe your salary can give you a stable life. So I left for a short period, but had to go back because I couldn't find any jobs in movies. At that time Hong Kong films were very good; everyone had a company, everyone I knew was making movies, but still I can't find a job. That's true! So I went back and made a TV series about the stock market, and this is a very important point for me, because the series was very successful and everybody knows that Lau Ching-wan is a very good actor just from that. When I

劉青雲

with Anita Yuen in
C'est La Vie,
Mon Cherie

read the script I thought it was the best script I had ever seen for television. Actors always have too many excuses, you know, "ah, the script is no good," but now I had no excuses. I said to myself: "You are on your own - if you can't play it good you'd better give up and die." When I finished the job I still did not know what would happen next, but the newspapers and magazines wrote about it and I thought this was a very good chance to leave; if I didn't leave then, no more chances. But I still can't find a job!

So I went to Taiwan - because Taiwanese television pays much better than in Hong Kong - even though I didn't really want to go because I wanted to get into the movies. But when I'm there I find I'm acting with another Hong Kong actor, Derek Yee Tung-seng, and I already knew him - when I was 18 a director had been looking for people to shoot a movie, and this was Derek Yee's brother - and when we went for a drink he started to tell me the story of **C'EST LA VIE MON CHERIE** and I told him, I thought it was very good story and if he ever had the chance to make it I would like to be in it. When I finished the TV program I came back to Hong Kong and I got an offer to join a movie for one or two days. My agent told me not to do it, but I am at the beginning. Movies and TV are different; I have to prove I can do it. So I went. Life is beautiful, sometimes! They told me that I have four days with the South African actor, N!xau, from **THE GODS MUST BE CRAZY**, and the producer discovered that the funniest things in the film were him and me, so I went from four days as a supporting actor and I went to South Africa and I think I was very successful in the movie. And then Derek Yee came back to Hong Kong and made **C'EST LA**

劉
青
雲

with Anita Yuen in
C'est La Vie,
Mon Cherie

VIE..., and I did it. It was important as it gave me more choice and people realised I can do both comedy and love stories.

*Can you explain the appeal of **C'EST LA VIE, MON CHERIE**, because many Western viewers just can't understand why it's so special.*

I think it's very local. It's a very old style story; the girl has cancer and falls in love with a musician. It has so many local jokes; they sing the opera, they still have Temple Street, exactly the same. So Hong Kong people can believe it actually happened; it's truth. It shows how people make their living, that it's hard, and that the people are poor, singing on the street, in the rain...
    And the very different thing for the female audience is that they think Anita Yuen in that movie is very strong; she faces the truth and can tell the guy "I love you." This is very different for a Chinese girl; that generation are still very old fashioned. If the girl tells you "I love you...." *(laughs)* In other countries they are very open. To say "I love you" is not that difficult, you know, but for Chinese girls...

How did you get on with your co-star?

Anita Yuen is very good. Perfect. So lots of girls love her! She is a very pretty girl with attitude. If she were here we can't speak like this, but she loves to talk and make everyone feel very happy. Of course, in the film I have to love her. We never call each other, so it's not like she's a friend, but if we meet we can talk privately...

劉
青
雲

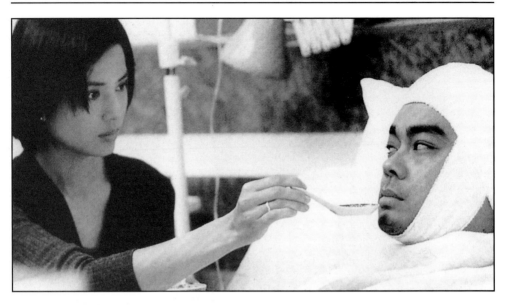

with Carmen Lee in
Loving You

She's an excellent actress but she makes so many films, some of which aren't so good. But this seems to be the way of things in Hong Kong.

In Hong Kong many people making movies always respect the old generation. Look at Wong Fei Hung, the actor Kwan Tak-hing, you know. No-one will say that he makes too many movies. But me, if I make seven each year, they say "too much!" I don't know why. Maybe because I'm still alive!

But I do have a problem and that is I can't stop. I can't stay in the home. My hobby is shooting movies. I really love the job. Many people say you have to choose the good one. But how? Even a good director or a good screenwriter can give you some shit. If I think, maybe it has a chance, then I will take it. Just like **C'EST LA VIE, MON CHERIE**. Nobody could tell that it would be a success. Many of Derek Yee's friends told him not to do it... that it will lose money. Sometimes I make bad choices, but you still have to do your best. There are so many mistakes, but this is life. You make a mistake and you think you will learn something and never do it again, but you will do it again and again. This is human being, right? If we can change, say if you have a bad temper, you will change many years ago. But when you're over thirty!...

*You worked for Tsui Hark in **TRI-STAR**, and had a beard.*

It was fake beard; it was Tsui Hark's idea. He wanted something different. He has many strange ideas. I dunno, maybe you can understand his jokes.

***LOVING YOU** is very impressive, especially taking the risk of making the character initially so unsympathetic.*

劉
青
雲

Poster for Tristar

Sometimes when you're an actor you have to give up the audience, because they're never satisfied. So the best way is to enjoy yourself first. In that film the most difficult thing was deciding, "What do you want to say? What do you want from that man?" The bullet [*Ching-wan plays the part of a cop who is shot in the head. He lives, but loses his sense of taste and smell.*]

Poster for **Big Bullet**

劉
青
雲

can change him in many different ways; so we chose that when he leaves the hospital he will feel something about life, because he was very close to death. But when he sees his wife with the other guy the anger comes back into his heart, the old memories return. So it's not that easy for him to clean up. In many movies a bad guy gets hit and changes into a good guy, but life isn't that simple.

Chinese always say man has two kinds of problems: money and women! But when we saw the movie again we thought we could have had a better ending; it would have been better if he can't face his wife again; that he still loves her, but some of the memories can't be cut out.

Can you talk about the audiences in Hong Kong?

About five or six years ago audiences really enjoyed Cantonese movies. At that time there were still the Taiwanese and Korean markets so people could make movies. But the producers always think about how to make them fast rather than how to make them better. And they're always very simple; that is, one plus one equals two. But I think the audience was getting smart. They went to the same school as me and you; we have the same IQ. So the audience starts to change and they can see the films are lousy. And then Hollywood movies come in with big budgets, and even the worst American movie is better than the best Hong Kong movie. So they start to say "if you still go to see the Cantonese movie you are a jerk!" That is exactly what happened. They just gave up on the Cantonese movie.

I think now would be a very good time to do something different. Something special. Many people have changed their jobs; they know making movies can't make much money anymore. So those still doing it are the people who really want to do it. And I think in the last year there have been good signs; that people like Peter Chan and Johnnie To are really doing something here. But the problem is the very small market. People are looking to the Chinese market but I don't think it's that easy. I think we'll struggle for a long time, but I hope we can

with Theresa Lee and Jordan Chan in **Big Bullet**

survive because Hong Kong movies are very different from those from other countries. I think we should try to use other countries' budgets. Ringo Lam and Tsui Hark went to Hollywood to shoot movies, so I think if the investors think the Hong Kong directors are good maybe we can use their money to shoot in Hong Kong.

LIFELINE might be described as the Hong Kong version of BACKDRAFT. It was done for a minuscule budget in comparison, yet is much more impressive in virtually every department.

You know **LIFELINE** had a budget of only ten/twelve million. This only happens in Hong Kong. This is the first movie about firemen in Hong Kong, and we have real fires! It's dangerous. This is the difference. In Hollywood the actor would not take these kind of risks. But we have to do it.

What directors other than Johnnie To do you particularly like working with?

Benny Chan is one of a new generation of directors and is one of the best. The first time I meet a director I ask him "what do you want?" We can talk to each other and create something.

Are you interested in directing yourself?

Maybe. Sometimes I think I'd like to do something of my own; my ideas. But I think the time is not right. I've talked to Johnnie To about this and if I have the story I can do it, but I think at the moment I don't have enough confidence. But some day.

劉青雲

Poster for **I Wanna Be Your Man**

What sort of films do you personally like?

Actually I find British movies very interesting; sometimes they're very different from Hollywood movies, **TRAINSPOTTING**, for example. Though in Hong Kong we don't see many British films. My favourite British film is **MELODY**. I've seen it many times; my sister saw it over ten times in the seventies. When I was very young and went to the cinema and saw the movie it was very sweet, and the audience was very quiet. When the film started they sang the song, the Bee Gees song. They all sang together. They knew all the songs from the movie. It's very touching. Hong Kong people like that sort of movie. If you saw the movie when you were a child you will love it forever; so when you grow old it will be in your memory. I remember going to see it with my brother and my first girlfriend.

Just like when we saw **GODFATHER PART 3**; the film is not that good but we remember parts 1 and 2 which we saw many times, so Michael Corleone's memory is my memory. So when we see part 3 all the memories come back.

Do you consider yourself an actor or an star?

Actor. I try to be a star but I cannot! I try to be an idol, but sorry. It's always better being a singer than an actor. You are always handsome, and you have so many screaming fans. You don't have to worry about the next location or what the director wants you to do; say, maybe, jump in the garbage! You do many disgusting things. But if you're a singer, you're always clean, always handsome, have so many girlfriends. I think the dream is very different, though of course, they have different pressures.

This is the reverse of the West where actors are more revered than singers.

Really? I have to go there! In Hong Kong nobody respects the actors.

You've been nominated several times but never won; what importance do you attach to the Awards?

I'd like to win before I die, so that when I'm old I have some memory. But they're not taken very seriously. The most important thing is making money. Anthony Wong said when he won, that the award is just luck. Not that he's not a good actor; but he's a very angry man with many complaints and problems.

What are you working on right now?

I'm now shooting a new action movie with Ringo Lam *[**FULL ALERT**]*. He is very smart; he understands everything in the movies including how to talk to the actors and how to deal with the producers. He's very clear. I think this film is also a bit different from what he's

with Wu Chien Lien in
Beginner's Luck

done before. Action is always important for him but with this film, he paid more attention to the characters. I act alongside Francis Ng. I play a cop and he plays the bad guy. We tried to put the good guy and the bad guy into the same situations, and give them the same problems. So the bad guy has a girlfriend, and although he needs to steal money he hates to kill people, and while the cop has to carry guns he hates them also. In many ways, we have the same feelings. So it's like I'm chasing my shadow. When the movie opens we talk to each other about killing guards before, and at the ending it's like "can we pull the trigger?"

Ringo Lam seems to have had an unhappy experience working in Hollywood.

In Hong Kong the director is the king; he gets exactly what he wants. You know, Hong Kong is a very strange and interesting place. If you want to find Hong Kong on a map you can find the name but the word is bigger than the place. But that place is very important for China and Asia. A long time ago when China was not that open, Hong Kong was the only door. From now on they open the market, but after they take back Hong Kong the next step will be Taiwan. They have to do it. Hong Kong is very modern and when we go back to China who will run it? It's very different from China and Taiwan.

劉青雲

*Lau Ching-wan
(centre rear) in*
Lifeline

Selected Filmography:

SILENT LOVE (1986)
CRAZY SAFARI (1991)
ANGEL HUNTER(1991)
ALL MEN ARE BROTHERS (1992)
EXECUTIONERS (1993)
THOU SHALT NOT SWEAR (1993)
C'EST LA VIE, MON CHERIE (1993)
IT'S A WONDERFUL LIFE (1994)
THE THIRD FULL MOON (1994)
BEGINNER'S LUCK (1994)
TEARS AND TRIUMPH (1994)
OH! MY THREE GUYS (1994)
DR. MACK (1995)
MOTHER OF A DIFFERENT KIND (1995)
TRICKY BUSINESS (1995)
HAPPY HOUR (1995)
ONCE IN A LIFETIME (1995)
LOVING YOU (1995)
ONLY FOOLS FALL IN LOVE (1995)
THE GOLDEN GIRLS (1995)
TRI-STAR (1996)
BIG BULLET (1996)
BEYOND HYPOTHERMIA (1996)
BLACK MASK (1996)
LIFELINE (1997)
FINAL JUSTICE (1997)
TOO MANY WAYS TO BE NUMBER ONE (1997)
FULL ALERT (1997)
MY DAD IS A JERK (1997)
THE LONGEST NITE (1998)

劉
青
雲

top:
in **Full Alert**

above:
with Michael Chow in **Third Full Moon**

right:
poster for **The Most Wanted**

ANDREW LAU

Born in Hong Kong in 1960, Andrew Lau Wai-keung has worked as cinematographer for some of the best directors in Hong Kong on some of the finest films that the region has produced during the past decade. His wide-ranging credits include Ringo Lam's **CITY ON FIRE** *(made in 1987 and in part a blueprint for* **RESERVOIR DOGS***) and* **WILD SEARCH** *(1989), Wong Kar-wai's* **AS TEARS GO BY** *(1988) and (with Christopher Doyle) the highly influential* **CHUNGKING EXPRESS** *(1994), the Tsui Hark produced live-action manga* **WICKED CITY** *(1992), and the Stephen Chiau comedy* **SIXTY MILLION DOLLAR MAN** *(1995). As such he has been instrumental in defining the look of Hong Kong cinema in the late eighties and the nineties.*

An attention to style is also the most prominent feature of the films he has directed, and his success as a director is evident in the box office figures for 1996, which show three of his films (the first three instalments of the **YOUNG AND DANGEROUS** *series) in the year's top 10 grossers. In January 1996 he co-founded the company BoB (Best of the Best) with Manfred Wong and Wong Jing which in its first year produced twelve films. These included the aforementioned* **YOUNG AND DANGEROUS** *films, which adapted from a Hong Kong comic strip, captured the high-speed, high-style lives of Hong Kong's triad youth, using a roster of new faces to create their own line-up of stars (and in Jordan Chan helping to establish one of the best actors of his generation). Lau was interviewed in BoB's bustling new premises in the month of the release of his then latest hit,* **YOUNG AND DANGEROUS 4***.*

How did you come to enter the film industry?

I started in the industry in 1981. I graduated from high school - it's hard to go to university - and I saw an advert in a newspaper from Shaw Brothers for a Production Assistant, which means helping out on the production, location scouting, that sort of thing. After three days I told the producer that I wanted to be part of the camera crew because when I was in high school I liked taking photographs, so the woman, who was very nice, called the camera department and I went there and became a camera assistant, just changing lenses, and after six months I became focus puller.

Chingmy Yau in
Raped By An Angel

Then later, in 1983, I went to New Cinema City - because even though I was learning a lot of things I felt Shaw Brothers was old fashioned - which was spearheading a new wave of Hong Kong movies, with good art directors, good cameramen (some from the States), and where I could learn new things from outside. Luckily in 1985 I got be a cameraman at Golden Harvest on **MR. VAMPIRE**. That was my first film. At first I was just the assistant but after ten days the cameraman went on to do another film. I was very lucky, because the director, Lau Koon-wai, also used to be a cameraman so I learned many things from him; he would tell me when he wanted a different angle or a different lens, and luckily the movie was nominated in the Hong Kong film awards.

Then I did another film for Golden Harvest and met Wong Kar-wai, and shot **AS TEARS GO BY**. The style of camerawork was very different because I wanted to drum out the old style; I used hand-held camera, and brought up the reds, blues and greens. I wanted the camera to show feelings. Because it was Wong Kar-wai's first time as director, he didn't know much about cameras or even the lenses, but he spoke his feelings. So I would try something and he would tell me if he liked it or not. I got another nomination, but every time I just get nominated; never win! But it doesn't matter.

When did you start directing?

*Maggie Cheung
and Andy Lau in
As Tears Go By*

I directed my first movie, **AGAINST ALL**, in 1989. At that time the bosses gave complete control to you, but unfortunately the script was not good. We can't handle the script; the company says you have to have certain things in the middle and at the end.

*For his second film as director Lau returned to the subject matter of his cinematographic debut, the hopping vampire, and directed Lam Ching-yin in **ULTIMATE VAMPIRE**.*

Then for Danny Lee's company, Magnum, I made **RHYTHM OF DESTINY**, with Aaron Kwok, and afterwards I went to Wong Jing's company and shot **RAPED BY AN ANGEL** (misleadingly retitled **Naked Killer 2** for some markets), for which the box office was quite successful. And the film's not so bad.

*After the supernatural comedy **GHOST LANTERN**, and **MODERN ROMANCE** (of which Lau directed one of four stories), Lau made **TO LIVE AND DIE IN TSIMSHATSUI** in which the treatment of the Triads in many respects anticipates the **YOUNG AND DANGEROUS** series.*

I do like **TO LIVE AND DIE IN TSIMSHATSUI** because I worked hard on it. In Hong Kong people tend to think the cops are no good. But sometimes they think the Triad is good, so they are interested in Triad society, and even though they may be afraid they also hear about some good things. The Triads don't want to be bad guys! They're often young and living in small houses and so they have to go out and they meet people demanding

劉
偉
強

Ekin Cheng and Wu Chien Lien in **Mean Street Story**

劉
偉
強

protection money and it rubs off on them; so it's the situation and the surroundings that turn them into bad guys.

Some people say in Hong Kong there are maybe one million in the Triads, which in the commercial world is a lot of people. So I think that's a lot of people to see your film, a lot of box office. And everyday they have stories. When they wake up they want to make money. That kind of people, they have to use their heads; it's not just fighting. They don't want to fight, because if they have to call a hundred people they will spend a lot of money. And the more money they have the more power. And of course there's good situations for romance as well, such as the bad guy chasing the good girl. So in the movie I try to show all their feelings and their friendship.

After that I shot **MEAN STREET STORY**. The camerawork is different from my previous films, not unlike the TV series **NYPD BLUE**. I tried to get those type of visuals. But of course the people don't like it. They say "too fast, I feel dizzy when I see the picture. " But I still want to make something new. So in **YOUNG AND DANGEROUS**, I make it slightly slower but still try to experiment.

You then had something of a departure by making a historical drama, **LOVER OF THE LAST EMPRESS**.

Chingmy Yau in
Lover of the Last Empress

It's very different. After **MEAN STREET STORY** Wong Jing asked if I wanted to do **LOVER OF THE LAST EMPRESS**. I thought, 'why not?'. When I was at Shaw Brothers I worked with Li Hangxiang as a camera assistant, so I knew about how he directed his Qing dynasty films. We spent a lot of money on the sets and costumes, but it was too rushed. They wanted it finished in one month so we did it all in Hong Kong, although the props are Qing dynasty. I wanted it to be better than Mr. Li! It looks very good and it was a good experience.

Some sources (including his official filmography) credit Lau as director of **I'M YOUR BIRTHDAY CAKE**.

With **I'M YOUR BIRTHDAY CAKE** I was just a cameraman helping a new director *[Yip Wai-man]*. He was my assistant, and the company wanted to make a change but I looked after him. The film is okay; I think you have to give the young people a chance, so if I can help them...

Chingmy Yau was nominated for a best actress award for the film.

She's very hard working. Of course, some people don't like her, but her attitude is very good.

劉偉強

Chingmy Yau in
I'm Your Birthday Cake

What made you decide to set up BoB?

Very simple. At that time, in 1995, I was working for the same company as Wong Jing, and we wanted to be able to spend more money on productions and shoot the way we wanted. But we had to find a partner in order to expand. We talked to a lot of people, but most of them just wanted to be directors. So we found Manfred who had a lot of experience.

*Was **YOUNG AND DANGEROUS** the first BoB film?*

You can say that. It brought the three of us together, though we used a different company name. When I wanted to do it a lot of people looked down on the idea and said "no-one will want to see it," and of course, Yee-kin and the other stars weren't very famous at the time. So we tried a number of new things and made it on a low budget - we only had a small amount of money from Taiwan and from the video company - but halfway through the shoot we could feel it would be successful. When we were on the streets, people showed a lot of interest. With the costumes and the acting I tried to make it look young, because it's the young people who go to the theatres. I tried to create a new look for the gangsters, like Yee-kin, who are good looking and dress expensively. Before we started shooting, I told the costume designers that I wanted a new look, even the hair styles, and after they saw the film a lot of people wanted to look like that. I also put a lot of songs in there; normally they just use one but we used five or six.

Were you worried that you might be glorifying the Triads as some critics have accused you of doing?

This is a very hot topic! But if you don't glorify them the film won't work. In my mind I just wanted to make a good movie and I always say, this is just a movie and it is from a comic, which is why I put so many comic shots in the middle of the film. So when they go fighting and people are killed I use these images to remind

劉
偉
強

people "it's only a film!" Some people think that I glorify the Triad, but I just want to make a good movie. But even though sometimes I may hate that type of person, in the movie you must like them, and make the actors feel like real heroes. I make a very clear distinction between good and bad. and the bad guys must die.

導演：劉偉強　　監製：文雋
主演：鄭伊健　陳小春　黎姿　黃秋生　邱淑貞　林曉峰　譚小環

Poster for
Young And Dangerous 2

In Part 4 there is a scene in which Yee-kin goes into a classroom and talks to the kids about Triad life, but seems resigned to the fact that they have no other future. How much are the films just entertainment, and how much message?

I try to do it softly. In Part 4 I'm trying to show that some people have no choice but to go in the Triads and once they're in they can't go back. I'm trying to say to the students, "don't go into the Triads", so I show how Yee-kin loses his friends, and how his girlfriend has been killed, but some people still say I glorify the Triads. Part 3 was more about the politics of the triad society, whereas in part 4, the final scene, for example, is quite political; a reference to 1997. Actually, in the beginning, the censor cut the film quite a lot, and it originally had a IIB rating; but now I put the stuff back in and it is Category III; it is now more political.

*Was **BEST OF THE BEST** [whose Chinese title promotes the film as a sequel to Gordon Chan's **THE FINAL OPTION**] a conscious effort to balance things out by making the Police the heroes?*

No. After **YOUNG AND DANGEROUS 3** I started another film [**THE STORMRIDERS**], a bit like **STARGATE**, but there were a

劉
偉
強

*Young And
Dangerous 5*

lot of computer graphics to be done, so we had a lot of time on
our hands, so I wanted to make another movie. But it was too
soon for a Part 4, so it was suggested I shoot a cop movie. At the
time there was a lot of SDU - the Special Duty Unit - in the streets
of Hong Kong, so we chose to do that type of film, because it's
easy to shoot. And I wanted to use some new people so we
found the young singer Chan Hiu-tung, and I also cast Karen
Mok because I thought she had worked so well in Part 3.

What lay behind the idea of using the Vietnamese as villains?

It was quite a serious problem. At that time it was on the news and
people were afraid of the Vietnamese. So it was a problem for the
Hong Kong people; it was topical. It was quite hard, because of
all the explosions, but the box office was not that good.

What do you think of the audiences in Hong Kong?

Some care, some don't. People react differently from England
where they respect the film and they don't have mobile phones!
When **YOUNG AND DANGEROUS 4** opened we like to go to
the midnight show because of the reaction of the audience. It's
a *real* reaction.

*Like Peter Hyams in the US you shoot all of your films yourself.
Why is this?*

Because when I first became a director, on **AGAINST ALL**, I
hired a cameraman and when we saw the rushes it wasn't what

劉
偉
強

Raped By An Angel

I wanted, so I took the camera myself because I know, but I can't describe, what I want. It's also faster; no need to talk! I didn't want to have to be telling someone what to do all the time. It's hard work, but it's better. So I shoot all my films myself.

What direction do you see BoB taking in the future?

We were supposed to make a big movie. **YOUNG AND DANGEROUS** now feels very raw and was very small but parts 2 and 3 become gradually bigger. In 1996 we started the Triad Society wave, so now in 1997 we try to start a new wave, using a lot computer graphics but in old age movies. We try to make good quality films, although we will still make small budget films with young directors,

So have the Triad films run their course?

Well, **YOUNG AND DANGEROUS 4** took HK$15 million, so I think I will make part 5 next year.

Filmography as director:

AGAINST ALL (1990)
ULTIMATE VAMPIRE (1991)
RHYTHM OF DESTINY (1992)
RAPED BY AN ANGEL (1993)
GHOST LANTERN (1993)
MODERN ROMANCE *[one episode]* (1994)
TO LIVE AND DIE IN TSIMSHATSUI (1994)
LOVER OF THE LAST EMPRESS (1995)
THE MEAN STREET STORY (1995)
YOUNG AND DANGEROUS (1996)
YOUNG AND DANGEROUS 2 (1996)
YOUNG AND DANGEROUS 3 (1996)
BEST OF THE BEST (1996)
YOUNG AND DANGEROUS 4 (1997)
YOUNG AND DANGEROUS 5 (1998)
YOUNG AND DANGEROUS: THE PREQUEL (1998)
THE STORMRIDERS (1998)

劉
偉
強

Poster for
Best of the Best

CLARA LAW

*with Joan Chen
on the set of
Temptation of a Monk*

羅
卓
瑤

*Clara Law Cheuk-yiu was born in Macau, and studied in Britain, at the National Film School, where she made her graduation film **THEY SAY THE MOON IS FULLER HERE** (1985), before returning to Hong Kong. There she met her future husband film director Eddie Fong (whose impressive resume includes **AN AMOUROUS WOMAN OF TANG DYNASTY** and **PRIVATE EYE BLUES**), and the two collaborated on the script for Law's Hong Kong debut **THE OTHER HALF AND THE OTHER HALF** (1987) a warm and perceptive romantic comedy dealing with the problems of married couples living apart due to emigration. It also represented her first collaboration with producer Teddy Robin.*

*She followed this with an atmospheric ghost story featuring Joey Wong **REINCARNATION OF GOLDEN LOTUS** (1989), the commercial success of which enabled her to make **FAREWELL CHINA** (1991), a searing drama set in New York about the horrors facing illegal immigrants, starring Maggie Cheung and Tony Leung Kar-fai. She compromised herself by directing the Leon Lai/Vivian Chow vehicle **FRUIT PUNCH** (1992) in order to be able to make the low-budget **AUTUMN MOON** the same year; the telling of a chance encounter between a young Japanese man and a Chinese schoolgirl in Hong Kong it is perhaps her best film to date. She then made something of a departure with the large scale costume drama **TEMPTATION OF A MONK** (1993), starring Joan Chen, and contributed an episode (as did Lizzie Borden and Monica Truet) to the portmanteau **EROTIQUE** (1994).*

*Her latest film **FLOATING LIFE** is the first film Law has made in Australia, where she now resides. I spoke to Clara Law the day after the 1997 HKIFF had ended, in the now abandoned press office.*

*Masatoshi Nagase
and Li Pui Wai in*
Autumn Moon

Miles Wood:

Can you talk about the importance of the time you spent in England?

Clara Law Cheuk Yiu:

I think even before I went to England my interest was in European cinema and some Russian and Japanese cinema, and I chose to go to England because I didn't know any other foreign language and I felt that was the place where I would feel closest to European cinema. I have never been very interested in American cinema, so that was the main factor affecting my decision. The school was a good training ground - it was mainly workshops - but the most influential part of my stay was where I lived I could go to the Electric Cinema, so I would be going there to see triple bills of Pasolini, Bergman, all the Europeans, and I think that was very good because when you can see a director's work in a handful like that you begin to see what it is about and appreciate the stages of development, and so you learn that way too. It was a stage; part of a chain of things.

The environment of living in London also had an effect, but not in a very positive sense. For a long time I felt very alienated and that was a big shock to me because I didn't realise that I would. I had studied English literature here in Hong Kong University and I was sent to an Anglo-Chinese school here which meant I was taught to speak and think in English as a kid - though I was brought up in a very traditional Chinese family - and I'd always thought I knew the English and their culture very

羅
卓
瑤

*Tien Niu and Gan Kwon Leung in **The Other Half and The Other Half***

well. But it felt very, purely, British and you feel you are not part of that, and for me it was like six months of living in a vacuum, and I felt I was not part of anything. Of course, it was 1982-5, and Margaret Thatcher and Dang Xioupeng were talking about the future of Hong Kong and I was very, very troubled. I was in that stage when I felt maybe I didn't have a place to go back to and all the students (twenty were British, only five were foreign) would finish and they were the cream; my graduation film was about the Chinese and BAFTA would sign up British but not non-British students, so there was no offer. But I had made up my mind to come back anyway; I never thought of staying.

*It was 2 years before you made your first feature **THE OTHER HALF AND THE OTHER HALF**.*

The script stage was in 1986/7. Before I'd left Hong Kong to study I had the offer to do a film; people had seen my television work. In fact, the producer had tried to talk me into going to London later, but I had decided I wouldn't because I wanted to start the course from the beginning, and so I refused. I thought I would come back to numerous offers *(laughs)* but of course it didn't happen like that, and you find when you leave Hong Kong for 2 years everything changes, so when I returned to Hong Kong the film scene was very different. Before I left it was still the beginning of the new wave and there was a lot of energy and hope, and when I came back a certain genre was taking a lot of money, and there was a lot of repetition, and the superstars had been created. So it was getting stagnant and there was a lot of suspicion about younger filmmakers. So it took me two years,

Tony Leung Ka Fai in
Farwell China

and I was lucky to have Eddie Fong - now my husband - who at the time was a scriptwriter that I approached to work with me on a certain project; though I told him we wouldn't get paid unless we got it off the ground, he was still willing to do this. So we finished the script and took it to literally all the producers and finally ended up with Teddy Robin. Eddie had made two films at the time and he served as Associate Producer, and Teddy always wanted Eddie to make sure I was doing the film in a commercial way!

What pressures were you under? For example, was the happy ending forced upon you.

You know that to survive there are certain codes you have to follow, and actually my early films were always trying to find that balance of doing things I wanted to do whilst not neglecting that commercial part. Otherwise you won't get the chance to make another film. If you get a flop, you are out! And luckily **REINCARNATION OF GOLDEN LOTUS** did very well, both here in Hong Kong and especially in Taiwan, and allowed me to do a film I really wanted to do, and that was **FAREWELL CHINA**.

FAREWELL CHINA paints a very harsh picture of New York. Had you been there?

Two times a year they would have the graduation screenings in BAFTA, and I finished my graduation film earlier than that

羅
卓
瑤

Reincarnation of Golden Lotus

screening. Other students hadn't finished so there wasn't a whole slot where they could show it, so I had to wait. In the months in-between I went to New York and worked there - legally! - in a cable TV station in Chinatown. I worked as an anchor, so I was in front of the camera for the news, but I also worked on a magazine programme which was like a profile on the successful Chinese in New York outside of Chinatown. So I came into contact with a lot of Chinese people and what they had encountered. And of course, when I worked on my graduation film in England I also did a lot of research with the Chinese in London.

*If **FAREWELL CHINA** was something you really wanted to do I hear **FRUIT PUNCH** was something you're not too happy with.*

羅
卓
瑤

I hated it! It was sort of forced on me, but I took because I wanted to make **AUTUMN MOON** and it was happening at the same time. But **AUTUMN MOON** was made for very, very little money - about US$200,000 - so that Eddie and I were working as directors, producers, and also we edited it. So we took a lot of roles for which we weren't paid and then we got people in who always wanted to work in more senior roles but didn't get the chance; so we got a gaffer to be the cameraman, for example; so he got an opportunity and it became his show-reel. So a lot of people worked because of that, and there was a lot of energy and a good rapport on set, but people weren't paid very much as it was made on a very small budget. So, in order to support ourselves we needed to find something more commercial that

above:
*Masatoshi Nagase
and Li Pui Wai in*
Autumn Moon

left:
Temptation of a Monk

we would be paid for. But I wasn't too happy and it was during this whole process that I decided I couldn't work like this anymore. I talked myself into doing certain things so that in **AUTUMN MOON** I was totally free and it was crazy. **AUTUMN MOON** was such as happy experience, it was such a contrast, I thought why should I make life so miserable for myself? And then **AUTUMN MOON** got a lot of success abroad so it opened up other doors.

So if other Hong Kong directors had similar experiences do you think maybe they would also reject the commercialism?

I don't know. It's a great temptation. In Hong Kong everything is monetary and you can make a lot of money if you don't find it so hard to sell yourself sometimes, and maybe some film-makers have that tendency anyway. So if they can make commercial films, why not? It's a matter of personal choice.

羅卓瑤

Actually, when I was doing **AUTUMN MOON** I was offered the chance to do a **YOUNG INDIANA JONES** episode for a lot of money. I turned it down, and since then I've had a lot of temptations but I keep fighting them because you have to pursue what you set out to do. Some were interesting, but I'm not ready for them yet. Maybe I would find that a relaxing time to have a luxurious ten months, first class travel and hotels but at this stage...

AUTUMN MOON *was one of a six film series entitled "Asian Beat"*

No, actually I overturned that. I was invited to Japan by the Japanese producer to this meeting of Asian Beat with all the other directors. I was very arrogant during that meeting. There was a proposal for Masatoshi Nagase to play a private detective and he would go to several Asian countries to solve a certain mystery. So one director from each different country would direct. But I thought that was crazy, totally ridiculous. We all have totally different cultures and would imagine Masatoshi as a totally different person in each country, so there would not be consistency in characterisation, and I think it's pretty boring anyway, so I said I think we should all have our own independent episode. Some directors were not fighting so much, but finally I got what I wanted; it was an independent episode. In all the rest he was a private detective, and they have all disappeared! *(laughs)* So I'm arrogant, but I'm right to be arrogant.

TEMPTATION OF A MONK *was a change in that it was a big scale historical production.*

It was financed by Polygram; Teddy Robin got backing from them to form his own company and that was the first project of the TedPoly Film Company. I worked with Lillian Lee before - she scripted **REINCARNATION OF GOLDEN LOTUS** - and she actually asked me to look at her book. It was a collection of short stories and there were 3 or 4 pages about a monk who felt very safe and then was visited by a nun who says "I was sent here to serve you," and he is very attracted to her, so he goes into mediation,

above and opposite:
Temptation of a Monk

fighting the devils, and it's a long battle but he wins. Then he hears a knock at the door and the nun reappears and it starts all over again. She asked if I was interested in making it into a movie. Eddie got involved on the third and final draft and I think it's an interesting project for me.

Joey Wong in
The Reincarnation of Golden Lotus

I should have been given more time. All the crew were in China; if we'd had more time for the script to be more mature and developed it would have been a better film. It would have been less direct. Every film you want to express yourself in a certain way and there are certain messages and if you have time to develop then that message becomes less obvious but stronger.

Was it successful in Hong Kong?

No, people find it hard to understand. It did well in Taiwan, though not as well as **REINCARNATION OF GOLDEN LOTUS**. Most of my films do well in Taiwan: they have a distance, and if I'm talking about the Chinese they can appreciate it but are not part of it. Tianamen is a bit far from them.

*How did **WONTON SOUP** come about?*

I was approached by an American company who said there were three women directors - at that time four - needed to do their own erotic pieces; the whole film is called **EROTIQUE**. They wanted totally different looks at eroticism and I found that interesting. I approached it from the point of view of what I felt eroticism was.

*You used Hayley Man from **FAREWELL CHINA** again.*

I discovered her in New York and she hadn't worked in any films.

羅
卓
瑤

Floating Life

She only did amateur theatre in Chinatown. She was very young, 16 or 17, at the time and I auditioned a lot of Chinese girls for the part in **FAREWELL CHINA** and she was the one I liked best, and thought about her again when I came to do **EROTIQUE**. She wasn't sure she wanted to be an actress and was not confident of her acting and always needed encouragement and wouldn't dare to look at her own rushes. She wanted to work behind the scenes, so she did a film course at USC.

*Does **FLOATING LIFE** show a solution to rootlessness; the ending in comparison to, say, **FAREWELL CHINA** is much more optimistic.*

Yes, I now probably feel more at ease with having two cultures in me, and living in Australia feels more like home. I can work there, which to me is very important, and I can actually take what I already have which is my heritage, the Chinese part in me, and bring it with me to wherever I go so... Because that world I was having longings for, that Chinese world, is a little non-existent anyway, it doesn't really matter where I am. The last two or three years I've become much more positive; I do feel that it's possible, and meeting with a lot of second and third generation Chinese and talking with them, people who don't have contact with their heritage, they have to come up with their own solution and they make good use of it.

It's also about a battle between trying to hold on to your own culture, integrating with the new or abandoning it altogether.

羅
卓
瑤

Annette Shun Wah in
Floating Life

I think you always need to find that balance and people walk their own path... if you try to negate part of yourself you will end up losing your balance. Maybe it's mental, maybe it's physical, but some part of you will have to deal with it in certain ways. In the film, Bing has a breakdown. Some people just feel ill. But if you don't deal with it, it will be like a cancer that grows in you. I don't think any culture is non-integratable, if there is such a word. I think it's really down to how confident you are, and how much you know of your own culture and that other culture. Take tea drinking for example, which is very much a Chinese thing, but which the British have a long tradition of too. So although it's a different approach I think there's always that possibility of finding common ground. And I like finding that common area, not just in culture, in people, in all sorts of things.

What lay behind choosing a middle-class family for **FLOATING LIFE**?

羅
卓
瑤

A lot of Asian immigrants, from Taiwan and Malaysia, when they immigrate to Australia or Canada, they are not poor. Of course, we have to distinguish between refugees and immigrants. But when you apply to go to Australia you need to meet a certain points system; you need to fulfil whether you speak English, have a profession, whatever. So immigrants are quite often well off. But the film is not about economic survival but that spiritual, mental barrier that everyone, richer or poorer, would have to go through. Of course, the poor in the beginning have to find survival needs, but after that they will still face the problem of finding a "place."

Leon Lai in
Fruit Punch

FLOATING LIFE *presents a fairly negative portrayal of Hong Kong in that it accentuates the frivolity of the place; the fact that people only think about stocks and shares?*

But isn't that true? We need to have the courage to admit what it is, otherwise you always live in something that's not real. So when people ask if I am a Hong Kong filmmaker - all these labels! - I say I don't care. I am what I am. And I think Hong Kong is basically a refugee camp: it was in the very beginning, and it still is, and people have to find a way to survive here. There have been different stages and we have a colonial government - and they don't want you to think, they want you to obey; to not make trouble - and the kind of education we are given is exactly that. And so the whole place tries to forget what politics is and concentrate on finding their own means of survival. Most people come here fleeing from a certain type of politics and the most successful people create the wealth and riches because they are so single-minded. Survival is very important when you're in a foreign place.

What is the major obstacle with making films in Hong Kong?

For me, the hardest thing when working on films here is there is no sense of culture. So people ask me is it because of politics that you leave Hong Kong, is it because of 1997, I think this is very simplistic. The whole activity of filmmaking here is a commercial activity. There has never been any Government support and there is no environment to nurture or support you to ensure that you, as an artist, grow. It just doesn't exist. So for me, if I find a place where I have more support then I go to that place.

羅卓瑤

For example Singapore, despite censorship, has realised that it must nurture creative people in order for culture to survive.

Yes, Singapore is maybe the next up and coming cinema. They are rich now and they realise when you're rich you need to establish your own identity or culture. Here in Hong Kong we've been rich for a long time but instead it's got worse! It's been going down in the last five years. In the early eighties we tried to deny that Hong Kong is a cultural desert, that there is water and more water, but now nobody even talks about that.

What are your current plans?

I'm working on a project entitled **GODDESS OF 1975** to be shot in Australia and, providing I can get the money, in Japan. It's about a Japanese coming to Australia to look for a car; his car is the goddess. Looking for the car is a pretext.

It continues the theme of cultural dislocation.

More than that. I'm moving on to other themes. One thing that interests me a lot is the dark side of human nature and I wanted to look into that. It's more deeply ingrained than **TEMPTATION OF A MONK**. When you describe a dark side you think of a dark corner, something secretive lurking in there and which you may not even be aware of. He's trying to find what it is. It's more about existence; a lot of dysfunctional family and relationships. For a long time we are faced with this loneliness and this indescribable despair, which is when the worst point is reached, and when we as individuals are given that power to do anything in the world - with science being a God - we are confronted with a lot of problems we are unable to deal with, both morally and spiritually. And that's something I want to explore.

What do you think the effects of the hand-over might be?

It's been shown, both in terms of censorship, and the way investment in Hong Kong films has been very short sighted. I don't think it will be very bright. I think Hong Kong people are very adaptable. That is good and that is bad, because if you're too adaptable you don't stand by your principles.

羅
卓
瑤

For me the less time I spend here in Hong Kong the more I can feel the change because I think that distance gives you a clearer picture of the whole situation and what it actually means, and I think that more and more I feel I don't know this place.

Filmography

THEY SAY THE MOON IS
FULLER HERE (1985)

THE OTHER HALF AND THE
OTHER HALF (1988)

THE REINCARNATION OF
GOLDEN LOTUS (1990)

FAREWELL CHINA (1990)

AUTUMN MOON (1992)

FRUIT PUNCH (1992)

TEMPTATION OF A MONK
(1993)

EROTIQUE (1995)

FLOATING LIFE (1997)

above and below: Temptation of a Monk
opposite: Clara Law

羅卓瑤

gigi leung

Gigi Leung in concert

I first encountered Gigi Leung Wing Kei in her role as Andy Lau's girlfriend in Derek Yee's 1995 film about illegal motorcycle racing on the streets of Hong Kong, **FULL THROTTLE**. Her understated performance displayed such subtlety and depth it was astonishing to learn this was her acting debut; one should remember though, that it was Yee who guided Anita Yuen to her 1993 Best Actress award in **C'EST LA VIE MON CHERIE**. After cementing her status as a rising star with a supporting part in the zany Stephen Chiau comedy **60 MILLION DOLLAR MAN**, she gravitated to starring roles in the popular youth movies of Joe Ma, which helped make her an "idol" of the fan-worshipping Hong Kong teenagers, while doing a complete about-turn and playing - with remarkable assurance - a gun-toting customs officer alongside Michael Wong in Gordon Chan's highly accomplished 1996 **FINAL OPTION**-prequel, **FIRST OPTION**.

1996 also saw Gigi recording her eponymous debut CD, which was followed in 1997 by her first Mandarin release, "Short Hair", both of which showed this was clearly not a case of an actress being pushed into an area best left alone. She has since released 2 more albums (one Cantonese, one Mandarin) and with her face constantly peering from magazine covers (on anything from "Marie Claire" to computer monthlies), the future looks even brighter now than when this interview was recorded. I spoke to Gigi backstage after a concert put on especially for her fan club (which showcased not only her singing but also allowed her fans on stage to participate in various games), an event that was attended by a packed house of teenage boys and girls who showered her with gifts ranging from cuddly toys and bouquets of flowers to expensive-looking necklaces and clothes.

路上的車
心上的人

在妳眼中我只是個自私的男人

爾冬陞 導演

劉德華 梁詠琪

烈火戰車
FULL THROTTLE

• 榮獲第一屆金紫荊獎（最佳男配角）
• 榮獲第十五屆香港電影金像獎（最佳剪接獎）

錢嘉樂 | 秦 沛 | 吳大維 | 徐錦江 | 柳影虹 | 夏 萍

ENGLISH SUBTITLES

Full Throttle

Miles Wood:
How did you get into the entertainment business?

Gigi Leung Wing-kay:
About two years ago when I was still studying at the Polytechnic of Hong Kong, one of my friends invited me to take part in a commercial, and when that advertisement was released the director of **FULL THROTTLE**, Derek Yee, tried to find me. And so that's how I started in films; he offered me a part in his movie, and from then people start to know who I am.

Was acting something you had always wanted to do?

No. I had never thought about it before. I took the part in Derek Yee's movie, simply because I thought it was a very good opportunity, with a good director, good actors and very good script. So although at that time I was still working on my design diploma course I tried to arrange my time so I could finish that movie. So after that movie I'm still thinking, am I going to carry on in the entertainment business or should I finish my studies. When I graduated I met my management company, Era, and I thought that they seemed a very good company and I could feel

梁
詠
琪

with Vivian Hsu in
We're No Bad Guys

that they were very sincere and had really good planning for me; it was not a case of just signing a contract and see what happens. They will push me. So I think everybody I met has been very good, because that's why I'm here!

How was it working with a celebrated film-maker, Derek Yee, and a major star like Andy Lau for your first film?

Actually looking back I don't feel satisfied with my part in the movie. Because at that time I was still a very new actress and there were some feelings I could not catch. For example, the character in the film is a girl 25 years old and who has been with her boyfriend for seven years; well, I have none of these experience before, so I think it was quite hard for me to show my sadness and just my experience in my eyes. Derek Yee taught me how to act. "Just act with your eyes," he said. "Don't act with your nose or your cheeks or your mouth. Because your eyes are your window. You can tell everything, even if you don't say anything. You just give eye contact, and if the audience understands what you are trying to tell then you are a success." So it was quite hard for me, but I tried my very best. As for the outcome, if I had the chance to do it now I think I could do it better. As for Andy Lau, well, he is a very hard working actor. He told me he sometimes keeps on working for eleven days and does not sleep!

They're making a sequel, only with cars rather than bikes. Are you going to be in it?

梁詠琪

No. It's a new story. It's not the same characters.

What was it like working with Stephen Chiau Sing-chi?

Oh, well he's really a very funny guy. When I saw him in a movie, up on the screen, I thought he was very funny, and he is very creative, and beforehand maybe I was thinking what is his real character? Because somebody told me he is very cool and he doesn't say anything to anybody and he just hides himself away. But after that movie I changed my impression of him; in his daily life he is still a very funny guy and he was very inspirational in our co-operation, and so I learned many things from him. And he is very easy to work with. He really works hard and so I believe he'll continue to be very successful.

with Daniel Chan in
First Love Unlimited

Joe Ma told me that he put a lot of his own experiences into ***FEEL 100%*** *and* ***FIRST LOVE UNLIMITED***.

I quite like Joe Ma's films because when I read his scripts I feel they are really my own experiences. Before he writes them he will have interviews with me, and get to know more about me, my family, my feelings about love, and then he writes the script. That's why when I acted in **FIRST LOVE UNLIMITED** I could think I was acting myself. That this was my story.

He likes to have interaction, between the scripts and the actor. He will find the most appropriate actor for the part. That why I feel I do really well in **FIRST LOVE UNLIMITED**. Because that's me. I can say that that's my best film, even though it's a very simple story, with no stars, no Andy Lau, no Stephen Chiau. I like the film very much.

You've packed some diverse roles into a short career, from schoolgirl experiencing her first romance in FIRST LOVE UNLIMITED to a gun-toting customs officer in FIRST OPTION. What's the criteria for choosing a particular part?

I chose the movies because they had good scripts, with very good directors. I've been very lucky, in that I have had the chance to do so many different roles. When you act

above:
Poster for
First Option

opposite:
television commercial
for jewellery product

in five movies playing the same character the audience will think you are like that, so I am lucky to have different kinds of characters. I enjoyed **FIRST OPTION** very much, especially as I've just done one action movie, and I liked Gordon Chan very much; he will not tell you things, he will ask you. Some directors may think "I am director, you are actor you must listen to me," When he met me, I was still a new actress but he asked me, "What do you think about this? What would you do next if you were really the character in the movie?" So he has a lot of democracy in his movies.

Joe Ma's films seem to have struck a chord with the young Hong Kong audience. Can you account for their success and maybe explain in what way they differ from other youth movies?

When **FEEL 100%** came out everyone thought it was very young and very fresh, and even older people, not just students but working girls also, would go and see this movie. I think it's because the things Joe Ma wants to tell are really happening; young people, teenagers, like labels like DKNY; that's real! So he does not try to skip these trivial things. He will keep them in and so when the teenagers go and see them they will see

with Simon Yam in **Hitman**

themselves and say "I will do that too!" and they will smile. So they like the characters, they identify with them, and they like the movies... You can say it's a bit too real because, for example, they will mention many labels, such DKNY or Money Exchange, in the movie. But that's really happening. People really pay attention to these things. It's really happening. I think that's normal.

How do you balance your acting and your singing? Which do you prefer, music or movies?

Actually, I will not try to choose one or the other, because so far I think I still have many opportunities in singing and movies, so I will keep on with both of them. But if you ask me which I like best then I will tell you I like singing more. Because, why did I start acting? Because I had the chance, so I started to learn. But as for singing: when I was very young, I learned how to play the piano; my mum took me to the Hong Kong choir and when I studied at Polytechnic I played in a band with my friends. So music is like my old friend, acting is like my new friend. I will try to keep very good relationship with both them.

梁
詠
琪

What sort of input do you have into your music?

I still have many things to learn. When I released my first album, it was quite popular and it won some awards. But there are still many, many ways for me to improve myself. But I don't have the time. If I do, I will find a teacher and learn singing every week. Because slowly you start to think you don't have enough things to give to people, to your audience. So I will push myself.

What are your ambitions, both in singing and acting?

In music, I would like to have my own concert not in AC Hall but in the Hong Kong Colosseum. I think it's the dream of every singer. But I have to keep on working hard. I need more experience, more songs, more fans. In both movies and in my albums I wish for improvement. That's important. I must tell myself that this one must be better than last one.

from her Photobook
"Gigi In Africa"

Filmography

FULL THROTTLE (1995)
DR. MACK (1995)
SIXTY MILLION DOLLAR MAN (1995)
FEEL 100% (1996)
FIRST OPTION (1996)
FEEL 100%... ONCE MORE (1996)
GOD OF GAMBLERS 3, THE EARLY STAGE (1996)
FIRST LOVE UNLIMITED (1997)
WE'RE NO BAD GUYS (1997)
HITMAN (1998)

梁
詠
琪

JOE MA WAI HO

Joe Ma

In 1996 Joe Ma Wai-ho built up a reputation that earned him the tag of Hong Kong's answer to John Hughes - that's intended as a compliment, by the way! - thanks to a group of films which successfully tapped into the youth market by accurately and sympathetically depicting the lives and loves, the dreams and fears, the joys and sorrows, of Hong Kong teenagers. In fact, the first and most popular of these films, **FEEL 100%**, was actually a reworking of one of his American mentor's movies.

But Ma's career amounts to much more than that; he has been a prolific writer working on all manner of films - from comedies like Johnnie To's immensely profitable New Year's outing **EIGHTH HAPPINESS** and Clifton Ko's **CHICKEN AND DUCK TALK** (both 1988) to action movies like Benny Chan's impressive **BIG BULLET** and Daniel Lee's comic-strip adaptation **BLACK MASK** (both 1996). His producer's credits include the 1997 Leon Lai/Sammi Cheng vehicle **KILLING ME TENDERLY** (the second HK remake of **THE BODYGUARD!**), and the serial-killer drama **NUDE FEAR** (1998) which he also scripted, and he has begun to develop an equally diverse résumé as director, with an episode of the portmanteau horror-comedy **TIL DEATH DO US LAUGH**, the Stephen Chiau comedy **LAWYER, LAWYER** and the, admittedly disappointing, reworking of John Carpenter's **STARMAN**, **HE COMES FROM PLANET K**.

初戀是最浪漫的，但亦是最易失敗的，

試問現今能開花結果的情侶當中，

有幾對是當年的初戀小情人！？

倘若第一次喜歡的人，便是能令你愛一生一世的那一半，

這是何等令人嚮往的美事！──但，

正因為它過於美麗，所以便只能在感覺的世界中存在嗎？

有人説

First Love Unlimited

Miles Wood:
How did you start writing for films?

Joe Ma Wai Ho:
When I was about eighteen I wrote a drama play for my middle school, for a competition, and it won a lot of prizes. A movie tycoon came and saw it at the theatre and thought it was great and asked me for the copyright to make it into a film, which in 1985 became **HAPPY GHOST**.

At that time I went into business as a research writer and then while I was studying at Hong Kong University I worked as a part-time script-writer. I graduated in 1987 and majored my career in script-writing for the first five years, and then I went to ATV to be a kind of creative director, and then went back to the film industry and started to try to be a director. That's a brief history.

Did you write many scripts before directing your first film?

Lots. An average of about five per year.

How happy were you with the finished films, and the treatment of your scripts by the film-makers?

Actually at that time I was young and every film was really just an experience. I cannot write a perfect script even now, so every

馬偉豪

*John Tang and
Eileen Tung in*
**Over The Rainbow,
Under The Skirt**

time I wrote a script, we'd discuss how to write a drama or how to make it comical, so it was a lesson. When I would see the finished movie in a theatre sometimes I'd think the director made it better, sometimes not. Actually, do you know Ko Chi-sum? He's the director of **HAPPY GHOST**. I collaborated with him on a lot of his movies and he was one of the best comedy directors in Hong Kong in the eighties. So he is my mentor, and I learnt a lot of techniques from him. He had a lot of input into the scripts; into visualising them.

Was directing something you were eager to do?

馬
偉
豪

Yes. In Hong Kong you must be very young to be a writer. Many people would come together to discuss the film, even the dialogue, so in the eighties the scriptwriter was often little more than a secretary, who wrote down what they say and think and try to organise them. And in most cases the writer feels very lonely; so when I'm twenty-four/twenty-five years old I thought to myself, "would I enjoy this kind of life for ten or twenty more years?" Because I want to see more people. Usually in Hong Kong the screenwriter cannot approach other crews because that's not his job, it's the director's or the producer's. So I thought it would at least be a good experience to open my eyes and my mind about the film industry, and if nothing else which will be useful for my script writing, such as how to make it practical in Hong Kong. So that was my plan. My first film was

Lau Ching Wan and ***The Golden Girls,*** *Ada Choi, Anita Yuen and Paulyn Sun*

called **RICH MAN**, a comedy about the very lower classes in Hong Kong, about 3 men, the *guo wak tsai*; you know the term? They are wise guys. Then one of them suddenly becomes rich because he accidentally meets a real rich man, and so starts living a different world. It was Category III film because of all the dirty words - the bad language. Actually, I don't like my first film very much, because it's just homework. People tell me to do that and I just fill in the blanks. So I don't think I can influence other people. Everybody has their own thoughts. Also the actors were thirty-five/forty years old, so they see you as a young idiot, so you are not able to be authoritative. It was just an experience, with a lot of mistakes, but actually the mistakes are very useful.

Was it commercially successful?

No, because I think the cast was not very attractive; just some ugly people who are not actually that funny, but it should be a comedy. So people do not come. Then I wrote some scripts while thinking what I should do next as a director and luckily I met Peter Chan, and he asked me to do my second film, **OVER THE RAINBOW, UNDER THE SKIRT** which is Hong Kong's **WONDER YEARS**. It's a film which I put a lot of my experience of growing up into; for example, the romance, and the relation with my family.

*Had you seen **YESTERME, YESTERYOU, YESTERDAY**, the first of Peter Chan's "rip-off's" - as he calls them - of **THE WONDER YEARS**, and did you like the television show?*

馬
偉
豪

Lawyer, Lawyer

Yes. Peter Chan introduced me to **THE WONDER YEARS**. Because **OVER THE RAINBOW...** is part 2 I have to use the same basic characters, but Peter told me to use my own experiences. Because as he said, for the TV series, every episode has different writers and different directors and they all put their growing up experiences into it. So I enjoyed it. For example, John Tang and his first love have a triangular relationship; that's my experience. It was quite successful.

*With **THE GOLDEN GIRLS** you got to work with Anita Yuen and Lau Ching-wan.*

馬
偉
豪

THE GOLDEN GIRLS is actually a remake of a Hong Kong TV series from the seventies. Actually I liked the TV series very much but it's quite "seventies" by which I mean men are superior to women, women fight for men and eventually they lose the men; that's the main issue. We made the film in 1995 so I thought in Hong Kong women's status has changed and they have more power, so we focused the storytelling on more powerful women who eventually get what they want. The TV series was quite bitter; very Cantonese language. "Bitter" is women's talk meaning "I dislike you, but I do not tell you." It's irony. But that's the culture of the Chinese women and in the seventies people didn't speak up or express their true feelings, so they built up anger in their hearts, and I think in 1995 people should speak up and be more Western and express what their feelings are. So the characters are quite different from the TV series.

Poster for *Feel 100%*

Ching-wan is very good, I like him very much, probably the best actor in Hong Kong, along with Stephen Chiau. Actually, I'm planning my next project with Stephen, and Eric Kot, a comedy set in the late Qing dynasty *[LAWYER, LAWYER]*. It's my first historical project, but I studied Chinese history in college so I know how to approach the material.

Sammi Cheng in
Feel 100%...
Once More

馬
偉
豪

Was the treatment of writers and actresses in the film taken from your own observations from working in the industry? For example the producers' refusal to cast the Anita Yuen character even though she is the best actress.

It's very funny because I shot the film for Win's company, which is a big company, and every day I would go in to discuss the cast and they always have a marketing angle to see creative works - they do say "she's more famous" or "she's more sexy" or whatever - so I put that into the script!

*So how did **FEEL 100%** come about?*

Actually it was also homework. The producer Man Jun, you know, Manfred Wong thought that a remake of a comic book was marketable. So he collected the stars and asked me to write the script and direct it. So I took the project. I did see the comic but I didn't take anything from it; just the names of the main characters. The main story is about a young lady who is in love with her best friend but doesn't tell him, and the guy loves many other girls and doesn't notice that his best friend is in love with him, and when he finally finds out she feels insecure and thinks if she goes to bed with him maybe he will then kick her out. So she doesn't accept him until he does something really romantic to please her and then they come together. I stole the spirit of John Hughes' **SOME KIND OF WONDERFUL**, but nobody realised; I loved that movie so much from when I grew up, so I tried to remake it.

The Golden Girls

And it was a big success?

Yes, in two senses. In the first it has quite good box office, and in the second it created four new stars. Yee-kin was famous before **FEEL 100%** for being a *guo wak tsai* in the film **YOUNG AND DANGEROUS** which was a big box office hit, but he hadn't played this kind of character, a modern Valentino. And the two ladies, Sammi Cheng and Gigi Leung, before it they weren't superstars in the film industry, but after they became very "in". And Eric Kot too. And that success is quite valuable because we need to have more actors and actresses.

    For the sequel I tried to do something different, because you cannot have a photocopy of the first movie, just within three months. **FEEL 100%** was released last summer and this was last Christmas. The concept is actually from **ST. ELMO'S FIRE** - A loves B, B loves C, C loves D. They mix their friendship with love. Yee-kin and Sammi live together but don't think about marriage and finally he walks out to have an affair, but finally realises he loves her and comes back. Actually it's more mature than the first one. Older audiences liked it more but those aged under twenty didn't like it; they want fantasy. **FEEL 100%** is fantasy, but the sequel is more realistic.

    The critics prefer it, as they think the first one is just ice cream; if you let it melt you are left with nothing. They think the second one is more like a cup of coffee; you can make it have feelings. But anyway the critics are all my friends!

*Can you talk about **LOVE AMOEBA STYLE**?*

I produced it. Neither the director - Shu Kei - nor I wanted to make this movie. We made it for the company, because they think it's marketable. But we don't think so, because it's too gimmicky for the audience. It's just a secondary product, though it is much more mature, so again the critics liked it but the audience didn't.

*When I saw **FIRST LOVE UNLIMITED** I immediately thought of John Hughes. It took a while before his films, which made a lot of money, became accepted and taken seriously by critics.*

In Hong Kong also the critics discriminate against these types of films. Because they're about young people they therefore think they must be childish and stupid, and just a waste of time.

FIRST LOVE UNLIMITED is quite original - the comic you can buy is only a side product - about a lower-class boy who falls in love with a middle-class girl. We put in a lot of lower class background, whereas **FEEL 100%** was quite bourgeoisie. The scriptwriter helped me a lot because I don't have the background of the boy, so he had a lot of input. The concept is a fantasy: you love one and you love one forever.

Gigi Leung is very good in it.

She's charming. She's very clever and smart, and after she reads the script she makes notes and discusses the role with me, which is a very good attitude for an actress. I think she needs a kind of breakthrough; in her next project she must do something very different, but I don't know exactly what that is.

Was it difficult making the sister a lesbian in a commercial film?

No, actually just the reverse; the topic is quite commercial in Hong Kong now. In fact, it's just a gimmick. **HE'S A MAN SHE'S A WOMAN** was a great big success and people in Hong Kong now accept gays and lesbians. At least on the screen!

*Although **A QUEER STORY** wasn't too successful.*

Maybe because of the casting. I don't know.

*You seem to have a habit of putting directors in your films. Allen Fong was in **THE GOLDEN GIRLS** and Edward Yang was in **FIRST LOVE UNLIMITED**.*

Two reasons. I love both Fong Yuk-ping's and Edward Yang's films, but how can I approach them? Well, Fong Yuk-ping is a friend of my producer on **GOLDEN GIRLS**, and Edward Yang is a very good friend of Shu Kei, so when we are thinking about the casting we just asked them. I think it's a little personal touch, which the masses won't recognise; they don't even know who Edward Yang is! But actually his outlook suits the character.

Did these directors influence you?

Fong Yuk-ping not very much because he doesn't plan his shoots, but Edward Yang yes, his movies impressed me very

馬
偉
豪

Stephen Chiau and Karen Mok in **Lawyer, Lawyer**

much. They have a very realistic feel. Ten years ago when I was in the Arts Centre as a student to see his movies, they were shocking to me; I couldn't imagine Chinese people can shoot that sort of urbanised city look, and which had such real depth. But I think I can never do that.

I like making fantasy for the masses. Maybe because as a writer at the beginning of my career I enjoyed sitting in the theatre and seeing the people around me are laughing. I find the atmosphere is very touching and I think for me the standard as to whether a movie is successful or not is how can you make them laugh and make them feel positive.

How did **FIRST LOVE UNLIMITED** *do at the box office?*

Okay, but not great because the casting is weaker. She is good, but he *(Daniel Chan)* is too new and many men don't like him, because he's too beautiful. They don't like beautiful boys, so they don't buy tickets. He's still immature; green and inexperienced. We discussed the script for a long time and tried to get something from him and make him feel involved, but he's very insecure; I always have to keep reassuring him.

So is this trend of youth films coming to an end?

馬
偉
豪

Anita Yuen and Eric Kot in **He Comes From Planet K**

Actually, I don't see it as a wave. I won't say it's the end of the youth movie because maybe another director can shoot more commercial and touching youth movies. But in the near future I don't plan to make any more, because I don't have any more experience to put into the films. Before you're boiled you must change.

What do you think of the current state of the Hong Kong film industry and the audience's treatment of the films?

The problem is that the market is too small. Most of the Hong Kong audience feel great pressure with the '97 issue, so when they go to the theatre they just want to buy fantasy. For example, Hong Kong audiences love **THE ENGLISH PATIENT**, which although it is more serious than Hong Kong movies it is also a fantasy about love and romance from different races and different people. You can shoot serious movies in Hong Kong but you have to package them, and that's a secret that I don't really understand.

Many Chinese in Asia love to see Hong Kong movies, but because of cost and time, although the theatre market is getting smaller and smaller, the software market - VCD, DVD - is expanding, so I'm still positive about filmmaking. But the way to enjoy a movie might be changing, with less and less people going to the theatre, that's for sure.

馬偉豪

Poster for *Over the Rainbow, Under the Skirt*

Filmography as Director

RICH MAN (1992)
OVER THE RAINBOW, UNDER THE SKIRT (1994)
THE GOLDEN GIRLS (1995)
FEEL 100% (1996)
FEEL 100%...ONCE MORE (1996)
TIL DEATH DO US LAUGH (1996) [one episode]
FIRST LOVE UNLIMITED (1997)
LAWYER, LAWYER (1997)
HE COMES FROM PLANET K (1997)

馬偉豪

shu kei

Director, producer, screenwriter, distributor, novelist, film critic. Shu-kei is all this and more. Born in 1956, he has made six films to date. There were long stretches between his debut **SEALED WITH A KISS** in 1981, **SOUL**, his excellent reworking of John Cassavetes' **GLORIA**, in 1986, and his Cantonese opera drama showcase for Josephine Siao, **HU-DU-MEN** (aka **STAGE DOOR**) in 1996, though the success of the latter may have ignited the directing bug in him, as it was quickly followed by two more films, and he also found time to script Chen Kiage's **TEMPTRESS MOON**. In 1990 he made a documentary about the Tiananmen Square massacre, **SUNLESS DAYS**, which was a prize-winner in Berlin. In 1986 he formed Creative Workshop, a distribution company which in particular helped focus attention on new filmmakers from China, Taiwan and Japan (with one of his most recent and greatest success stories being Shunji Iwai's **LOVE LETTER**).

      Sitting on the floor in a corridor of the Administration Building of the Hong Kong Cultural Centre, Shu Kei spoke with enthusiasm, passion and clarity not only about his own films but about Hong Kong cinema in general.

Miles Wood:
How did you start out on your life in film?

Shu Kei:
I started writing reviews in my high school days, which was around 1974, and I continued until 1976 when I was in my second year at University and I started writing scripts for television. At that time there was a group of young film-makers who came back from abroad having studied film in Texas or California or London and almost all of them went into TV and started making one hour drama episodes on 16mm. I started writing scripts for directors such as Patrick Tam, Yim Ho, and Ann Hui, and after graduation I became Yim Ho's assistant director and scriptwriter, and he then made **HAPPENINGS**.

      This was quite rare at the time, because it was youth film in the tradition of **REBEL WITHOUT A CAUSE**. At that time there were two films with similar subject matter and treatment; one was Yim Ho's film and the other was Tsui Hark's **DANGEROUS ENCOUNTERS OF THE FIRST KIND**, also called **DON'T PLAY WITH FIRE**. I think Tsui Hark's film is more complicated in a sense because it mixes in elements of politics whereas Yim Ho's film is more straightforward in its treatment of the rebellious young people.

舒
琪

Shu Kei

The whole film took place in a single night. At the beginning you have four or five youngsters roaming about the streets without any purpose at all, and then they steal a car and the whole thing keeps on snowballing until they commit murder and are on the run from the police, and the world is shocked. It's very violent, especially near the end.

Can you talk about your first films as director?

SEALED WITH A KISS is a love story between two slightly retarded kids. It was done when there were almost no love stories being told in Hong Kong Cinema. It was the rise of Cinema City and Tsui Hark and I think it was released at the same time as **ALL THE WRONG CLUES**. At that time there were only action films, kung fu films and comedies of the sexes. In retrospect the film was very juvenile, but at the time all I wanted to do was make a very, very pure love story and the fact that the characters are mentally retarded made it more pure, more innocent. But that was a big flop at the box office and for survival I had to do different things. So I started working for the film festival; I worked on the Hong Kong retrospective section for two years, and began discovering a whole legacy of melodramas and independent cinema in the fifties and sixties. After that I joined the film company D&B and became head of publicity. Two years later I made **SOUL**.

Deannie Yip in Soul

*Christopher Doyle shot **SOUL**.*

Yes. John Sham, who was in charge of D&B at the time, produced **SOUL** - he had also been producer on **SEALED WITH A KISS** - and it was done solely because I had great admiration for the veteran actress Deannie Yip. She had a very small part in **SEALED WITH A KISS**, and it had always been my wish to work with her and write a script especially for her. And the idea of a story very much inspired by **GLORIA** came to mind. So I wrote the script and asked John to produce it.

Looking back I think these first two films may have subconsciously been made as using film as a critique of the current cinema and trends of the time. With **SEALED WITH A KISS**, even the kung fu films or comedies rarely had even a convincing or believable romantic subplot, so that was made as a contrast to the trend. And **SOUL** was made because I was fed up with the formulaic filmmaking at the time. I could always tell what would happen five minutes into the film; everything was done according to a formula. So it was a mix of different genres: it started off as a thriller, then it turned into a melodrama, then into a comedy, then into a kind of women's film. I must say the storyline is very meandering but I structured it so people could not tell what would happen next. By doing that I was working in a way very much against the audiences expectations, and as a result it also turned out to be a big flop which explains why I did not do any more films afterwards for the next five or six years!

So you began distributing films.

Happenings

I set up Creative Workshop about eight or nine years ago. It stemmed from the same urge that made me want to write about films; the same love of the cinema. When I see a film I like very much I want to tell people about it and hope they will enjoy it as much as me, so when it became economically viable... I started buying and distributing when I worked for the film festival and society. For me distribution seems very natural.

*You went back behind the camera for **SUNLESS DAYS**.*

SUNLESS DAYS was a project commissioned by a television company in Japan - I started my association with Japan when **SOUL** was acquired for video and theatrical release, and became a kind of cult film there - who were developing a series of documentaries about various Asian cities and they wanted each episode to be directed by someone from that city. So I was asked to make a one-hour documentary on Hong Kong, and I submitted a proposal to do a film on the Taiwanese rock singer/songwriter Hou Dejian who defected, quote-unquote, from Taiwan to Mainland China via Hong Kong. So it was a very interesting case. It's very rare for someone to go from a free country to a Communist country via another free city. But it was 1989; they passed the project. All of a sudden there was the pro-democracy student movement taking place in China and then the June 4th massacre and he actually played an important part near the end. On June 4th he simply disappeared from sight and no-one knew if he was alive or dead. He was one of the last people to be seen on the square and he was also one of the four people just before the troops went in to Tianamen Square to

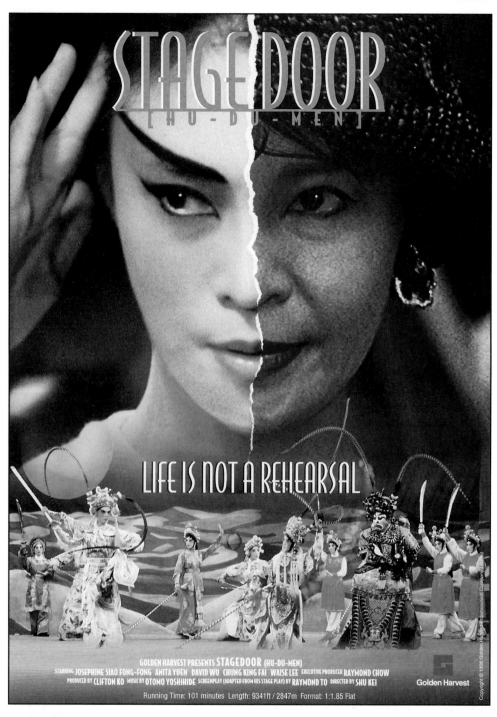

Poster for
Hu-Du-Men

negotiate on behalf of the students to let them leave the square peacefully. The company were very eager to do the film, because of the impact of the massacre. I was personally, like all Chinese all over the world, very shocked, and I proposed to do a film about June 4th and its effects on the Hong Kong people. I wrote a very rough treatment in which I proposed to do interviews with people in Hong Kong, all of them either close friends or members of my family, and they passed it immediately and started filming with a small crew covering Singapore, Taiwan, Australia, Venice, London, Canada. It's actually more a personal essay than a documentary looking at the influence of June 4th on these people's live's.

After **SUNLESS DAYS** there were several projects I wanted to do. None of them were realised. I saw the original play of **HU-DU-MEN** around 1990, and at that time after the trauma of Tianamen Square and **SUNLESS DAYS** I was very attracted by not so much the optimism, but the high level of energy and the very positive attitude of the female lead towards life. I immediately started talking with the playwright, Raymond To, and I had a producer who had worked on **SOUL**, and she agreed to do the film, so we optioned the play and contacted Josephine Siao Fong-fong, and it was interesting because at that time she was like the character in the film and was about to retire and emigrate to Australia. We asked her to do the film and she was delighted to do it and even postponed her emigration. Later she did go to Australia, but then moved back to Hong Kong. We discussed it a lot but when we were about to start writing the script the producer told us she had go to Canada on personal business and asked me to wait. I said "okay", as she'd already paid some money for the option, but I waited and waited and she simply disappeared! I think she emigrated but simply did not want to tell us and to this very day I've still heard no news from her.

So I put everything on the shelf until some years later Raymond To had two huge hits with his play adaptations, **I HAVE A DATE WITH SPRING** and **ONE OF THE LUCKY ONES**, and so I had the chance to revive the project, and Clifton Ko who directed those two films agreed to be my producer.

I liked the play but not because of the opera. I have very few experiences of watching Cantonese opera, so I'm not a die-hard fan, but I do like the colours and whenever I have the chance to see it I do enjoy it very much. But I knew very little about it until I started doing research for this film together with Siao Fong-fong. But it was the role she played that attracted me; it was very rare to find such a strong female lead.

*What made you decide to direct **A QUEER STORY**.*

A QUEER STORY was an interesting experience in that there was very little difficulty in getting the film done. It was not my idea to do the film. A friend of mine and another company brought the idea to me. The original idea was very simple: about a middle-aged gay man who decides to come out because he cannot hide it anymore, and my friend proposed the idea to his own company, but it was rejected. We discussed it a lot. It seemed quite a stereotyped and conventional way of doing a gay film and I always try to stay away from it, so it was quite ironical.

I was attracted to the idea because I thought we could do it in the form of a comedy. **HU-DU-MEN** was my first try at comedy; though you might term it comedy-drama, it had far more comic elements than my other films. Both in this time of my life and this climate - by which I mean the state of Hong Kong society - I would prefer to do comedies rather than heavy films, not because I wish to console the people but at this hour there is a lot of anxiety, insecurity, and uncertainty at the eve of the hand-over. This is a hard fact of life; something we cannot change. I personally don't reject it because it's bound to happen and I wish to aspire to a positive way of thinking in both my future career and the future of society, and I think it is pointless and senseless to express an irrational kind of uncertainty, frustration, or pessimistic attitude in any literary works. So it appealed to me to be able to deal with the theme of homosexuality under the shelter of comedy, which also seems to be the only way to get the finance for such a subject matter. When I presented the idea to Clifton Ko he liked it immediately and got the green light from Golden Harvest a few months later.

But after I made it, it's a different story. Golden Harvest expressed quite openly that they didn't like the film at all. To be precise, they hated it, and also the reaction to the film was quite unexpected to me. In general, I think the film played well with young people who are more liberal and open and for whom there are no inhibitions. But for more mature audiences, especially among the critical circles, it seemed to have created a whole lot of controversy. The revelation to me was that to the more mature and respectable circles the theme of sexuality - not just homosexuality - seems to be very much taboo and makes them uneasy. And I think for all its directness and straight-forward narrative the film was being criticised for being hetero-phobic, *and* that it also does more harm to homosexuals. It was a great surprise.

You followed this up quickly with **LOVE AMOEBA STYLE**. *Can you explain the title for those who don't know.*

LOVE AMOEBA STYLE is a quickie, in the sense I was setting up a company with Joe Ma, who made **FIRST LOVE UNLIMITED**, and we were offered by the exhibitors a golden slot during Chinese New Year. Policy-wise for a new company, it's an offer we can't refuse. The only thing is we had to rush out a film in the tradition of Joe's two hits **FEEL 100%** and **FEEL 100%... ONCE MORE** which are romances for young people. And Joe didn't want to direct it since he'd already done two of the same kind and I was the only other director in the company so I decided to take up the challenge of making a film in such a short time. So we started from scratch, and built a plot around the young cast, which also appealed because **HU-DU-MEN** and **A QUEER STORY** were sophisticated films, and working with

舒琪

the young actors in **HU-DU-MEN**, and Jordan Chan in **A QUEER STORY**, made me think it would be fun. The film was written as it went along; I was writing until the very last hour of shooting and we did it in eleven days. It's a comedy-drama about friendship, rather than romance, between the young. There's a magazine called "Amoeba," which is probably the best magazine for young people, and it captures the trends and lifestyles so it appealed as a label.

Andy Hui, Cheung Chi Lam and Eric Kot in **Love Amoeba Style**

What do you think are the specifically Asian characteristics of Hong Kong cinema?

I think it's difficult. Most Asian countries are Westernised to a large extent. Maybe Hong Kong films are more hybrid than other national cinemas, such as Japanese or mainland Chinese. I don't know what is an Asian quality, but I think Hong Kong cinema is determined not only by the nationality and character of the people but also by the geography of the city. So Hong Kong cinema is defined by a very condensed and concentrated geography which results in a lack of space and a speeding up of the rhythm. It has less expository scenes than other cinema and that is a result of the high-speed rhythm of Hong Kong life and the city operating at such a high-speed level. At the same time there are special operations and systems which determine a style which is entirely environmental or objective. We had a system of what we call the "Midnight Show" starting in the seventies; I can't really recall how it all started but I think it's in part a reflection of the economy and richness of society when all of a sudden people start to immerse themselves in a lot of night life. So we start the midnight shows at

舒
琪

above and opposite:
Ashes Of Time, *produced by Shu Kei*

weekends, where new films were being previewed on the whole cinema circuit at 11:30. And this became a kind of regulated system and the film-makers started to observe and use the reactions of the audience to determine the way they are going to revise and edit their films when they start the official run the following week. And this is very interesting because most people who went to the midnight shows were of the lower strata of the population and their reaction is very, very straightforward and what they are looking for is mostly pure sensationalism. And at the time the most popular films were kung-fu movies, and kung-fu comedies, and as a result the whole rhythm of the films was accelerated because these people are very impatient and whenever the film slowed down they would shout and yell at the screen. And having found out that the directors and even the stars were among the audience - it became a very common practice for publicity for them to appear at these sneak previews - and they would shout out insults if the film did not please them enough, so producers started to develop the habit of trimming the films according to the reactions of the audience at the midnight shows. Whenever they came to expository scenes or more emotional scenes the producers realised this would not work for the audience. So it became common practice for the filmmakers to go to the midnight shows on Saturday, have a production meeting on Sunday, and immediately start re-shooting new scenes or re-editing the film on Monday, and the film would then open on Thursday. Of course, this is a completely crazy thing to do, and as a result the directors would bear this in mind when editing the film, and therefore the fast rhythm became the golden rule of Hong Kong cinema, and this turned into the norm, especially when Tsui Hark developed a very high speed editing

舒
琪

Poster for
Hu-Du-Men

style. Another reason for this rollercoaster-like rhythm or style is that in the seventies almost one-hundred-percent of the Hong Kong films were shot post-synch. And anything without sound is an entirely different experience from anything with sound. Editing with sound you would realise film can be slowed down a little, and you can play more with the rhythm of not only the sound but also the visuals. Actually, the sound slows up the rhythm of the visuals. But without it you tend to do everything in a very fast way, and I think this is something that is very subconscious that the filmmakers do not realise.

Is there an alternative to this kind of cinema?

I don't think we have a tradition of art house movies. For example, there is a film starring Jet Li and Josephine Siao Fong-fong, **FONG SAI YUK**, which is a very commercial film for Hong Kong cinema, and indeed was a huge hit making more than HK$30 million, but when the film was shown at festivals, arthouse distributors in European countries picked it up and released it at arthouses because it was treated as a different type of cinema; a rare example of Hong Kong cinema. So I think it's entirely a matter of different perspectives. No Hong Kong film director, even Allen Fong, would claim his films are "art films", although maybe secretly he would admit to that label, but no-one would dare or would be delighted to call their films art films. Wong Kar-wai's films are shot in a very different style, are packaged; **ASHES OF TIME** has such a huge cast and all the actors are so popular it's just a commercial film with a different style.

Is the future bright?

How the future will change no-one can answer. I can only say I hope for the best. I don't think the worst will happen and I sincerely don't believe Hong Kong will be thrown back to the China of the sixties, or that censorship will become as strict as Beijing. I think the Chinese Government will try to keep Hong Kong under the umbrella of one country, two systems. There are bound to be changes but what kind it is difficult to say. So I think the best way to deal with it is to stay and work. I don't see any point in seeing the hand-over as a deadline; I think it's ludicrous to see Hong Kong as being completely turned over after July 1st into a dead city. Lots of journalists ask will there be a festival next year, will it be difficult to talk to you? To say I'm immune to this insecurity would be untrue but if you look at the development of China, things have been changing all the time and I sincerely believe Hong Kong has a very unique position, and the global development of Hong Kong will prevent drastic change. You may even say Communism is no longer Communism in China; they're learning to adapt to the world, though they're still very stubborn. For me the most worrying thing is not whether the new Government is going to impose a whole new set of laws or strict rules on the festival or even society, but rather the unwillingness or total conformity of the people; the policy making people working under the new Government, or those in the press and the media. Already there seems to be a trend of self-censorship, a softening among the press. This is the worst thing that can happen.

Some people seem to looking to the Chinese market as the saviour of Hong Kong cinema.

I don't think it will be open. Even if it is there is a long way to go before they establish an efficient system of distribution by which you can actually collect your revenue. There have been Hong Kong and Western films released in China but even if it is a mega-hit you only collect a small proportion. And there is still the competition of Hollywood.

Filmography:

SEALED WITH A KISS (1981)
SOUL (1986)
SUNLESS DAYS (1990)
HU-DU-MEN (1996)
A QUEER STORY (1996)
LOVE AMOEBA STYLE (1997)

Johnnie To

ALL ABOUT AH-LONG

もう一度、あなたと夢を追いかけたい。

CHOW YUN-FAT
SYLVIA CHANG

過ぎゆく時の中で

Japanese advertising for All About Ah Long

杜琪峰

Johnnie To Kei-fung is a filmmaker whose work, if not his name, is probably familiar even to those Western audiences with a just passing interest in Hong Kong cinema; he directed, or to be more accurate co-directed with Ching Siu-tung, the 1993 super-heroine feature **THE HEROIC TRIO** and it's sequel **THE EXECUTIONERS**, both of which, thanks partly to the shrewd casting of the "trio" of Maggie Cheung, Anita Mui and Michelle Yeoh, have become cult favourites in the West. But few will be aware of the sheer breadth and variety of To's filmography, which embraces comedy, drama, action and martial arts; indeed, it may have been the problem of tying To to any specific genre that has prevented viewers from fully discovering, and critics showing full appreciation of, one of the region's most accomplished directors.

Three times - in 1988 with the all-star comedy **EIGHTH HAPPINESS**, in 1989 with the Chow Yun-fat/Sylvia Chang motorcycling melodrama **ALL ABOUT AH LONG**, and in 1992 with the Stephen Chiau farce **JUSTICE MY FOOT** - he has directed the highest grossing film of the year. His work as a producer is no less impressive, highlights of which include Benny Chan's classic doomed-relationship movie **A MOMENT OF ROMANCE** and more recently a number of stylish and energetic films from young directors, including Patrick Leung's icy thriller **BEYOND HYPOTHERMIA**, Wai Kar-fai's highly inventive **TOO MANY WAYS TO BE NUMBER ONE**, and Patrick Yau's abstract, suspenseful **THE LONGEST NITE**.

Johnnie To was interviewed in the offices of his Milkyway Image company.

Stephen Chiau in
Justice My Foot

Miles Wood:
How did you start in the film industry and tell us about your first film.

Johnnie To Kei-fung:
The first film... I'll start with how I came to make the film first. I joined the television company TVB in 1972 as an office assistant. Then I found that I was very interested in producing a TV series, so I joined the actors training course held by TVB. After that, I worked as assistant producer - which included script writing and directing - in the company.

I made my first movie in 1978. The film was shot in the northern part of Guangdong Province, China. That film made me realise that I did not yet have the ability to direct a film, but the experience had great bearing on my career. So, after that I went back to TVB to work as a producer. It was not until eight years later, in 1986, that I made my second film, and I've worked in the film industry ever since. I don't know the English title of the movie. It is a comedy about ghosts.

*Tsui Hark is famous for being a difficult producer to work with. Can you tell me about the experience of working with him during the shooting of **THE BIG HEAT** which is one of the very best of the violent action films that followed in the wake of **A BETTER TOMORROW**.*

杜
琪
峰

directing Anita Mui and Stephen Chiau in Justice My Foot

I like Tsui Hark both as a director and a producer very much. But, thinking back about it, there was a communication problem between us, because I sometimes couldn't catch what he wanted. As a producer, he didn't always say and express his ideas clearly or tell what he was thinking. This may stem from him wanting to give room to the directors, but it lengthened the production time. Sometimes, after seeing what you had done, Tsui was not satisfied with it, and it was only then he told you what he wanted, and sometimes *he* made it again, and only then you realised what he'd wanted.

I was not very satisfied with the film and the box office is not so good in Hong Kong, although I know that Westerners like it very much. Well, this might be caused by the different attitudes and ways to watch a movie between Hong Kong and the West. But the experience with Tsui Hark did make me learn many things about film making.

*You then directed Chow Yun-fat in **EIGHTH HAPPINESS**, which was not only the highest grossing film of the year but won best film at the Hong Kong Film Awards.*

But that was a bad film, although it was a great success in box office. It was made for the Chinese New Year holiday. Chow played a *sissy* person and this was kind of a risk at that time, but it turned out the audiences accepted this and the box office was very, very good. However, I don't think the film is good. But yes, the success of **EIGHTH HAPPINESS** absolutely helped me to get full control of **AH LONG**. The production cost of **AH LONG** was

杜琪峰

only 6 or 7 million while the revenue of **EIGHTH HAPPINESS** was over 15 million. So the company had nothing to lose.

*How did **ALL ABOUT AH LONG**, which is a very strong emotional drama, come about?*

The idea first started with the old song "Tell Laura I Love Her" although the main character played by Chow Yun-fat was much older than the young guy in the song. So I changed it a bit and treated it as kind of flashback of him; I wrote that he didn't die in the car racing accident but his wife left him because of this. After eight years, she came back and wanted to take away his son. Chow knew that the break-up was all his fault, and even though he loves his son very much, he knew that he couldn't give his son a better life than his wife, and so he gave him to his wife. I didn't do anything to make the film any less, or any more dramatic or sentimental. I did it in a rather straight-forward way and just put in what we thought should be in the story. Chow and Sylvia Chang both helped in the script, they both wrote their parts in it, so they understood the script fully. This was the first movie that I had control of the story, the budget and the artistic approach. It gave me very, very, great satisfaction.

Lau Ching Wan in
***The Longest Nite**,*
which was produced
by Johnnie To

So was there any pressure on giving it a happy ending?

I never thought there would be an happy ending. It was because Ah Long had been wrong all through his life, that I didn't think he deserved a happy ending. As an artist's motivation, it was not a good decision, but I did think that Ah Long should not have a happy ending.

Yes, the ending feels right but it is unusual for a Hong Kong commercial film to have such an ending.

For the last scene, the car racing, the artist, Mr Chow, I thought, should face his destiny. Though, logically, it was not right.

*Both **THE HEROIC TRIO** and it's sequel **THE EXECUTIONERS** were very popular in the West. Why did you make these two movies and why did you make certain changes for the second one.*

杜琪峰

above:
Michelle Yeoh in
The Heroic Trio

right:
scenes from
The Heroic Trio

杜
琪
峰

Making **THE HEROIC TRIO** was a result of market consideration. I don't mean that we thought it would have a good box office. It was just that action movies were very popular at that time in Hong Kong, and the distributors in other Asian countries liked action movies too. However, male kung-fu actors are very hard to get; Chow Yun-fat, you know, doesn't really know kung-fu. Jackie Chan and Jet Li are both Golden Harvest's exclusive, Andy Lau also. Actually, nearly all the male actors have contracts. And then we, I and Ching Siu-tung, thought that an action film

need not necessarily use just male stars; action scenes using actresses could be good too. Therefore, we decided to make a film about three women.

At first we wanted to have a remake of an old Chinese film called **FEMALE FLYING THIEF NIGHTINGALE**, but when we were preparing for it, we found out that someone else was already re-making it [this became **DEADLY DREAM WOMAN**]. Since we wanted to have a serious production, with a well written story and production - and they started filming before us and we knew that we were way behind them - we thought that it would be meaningless to remake an already remade film, so we changed the story and made the **HEROIC TRIO**, a story about three heroines in an unknown time and place.

Mad Monk

In fact, the reason why we produced the second one was because the budget for the first one was very high and we needed to make two films to cover the whole production cost. Therefore, the making of the second film is kind of a must; if not, the budget could not be a balanced one. That was the reason why the action scenes, the ideas and the story of the second one were less creative than the first one, and this was also why there were less action scenes and more dramatic ones than the first one.

Both films were co-directed by you and Ching Siu-tung; how did this work?

This was not the first time I worked with Ching. Our co-operation dates back to the eighties when we were both in television, and we worked together on several films before these two. But this was the first time we were the investors and co-directed the films too. Ching was responsible for the action scenes and I was responsible for the story, and the pre- and post-production. Maybe due to the long working relationship between us, at the production site, we easily divided the work between us and it seemed like we were two-in-one. That is, the crew were only facing one director, not two, so they knew who to ask when they had problems concerning the different areas. Of all the people I've worked closely with or co-directed with, Ching is the best one.

杜
琪
峰

Aaron Kwok in
The Barefoot Kid

*Was **THE BAREFOOT KID** conceived as a homage to Chang Cheh's martial arts films of the seventies?*

THE BAREFOOT KID is actually based on a old Shaw Brothers film from the seventies *[Chang Cheh's **DISCIPLES OF SHAOLIN** (1975)]* of which I liked the story. The main character starts out barefoot and though by the end he's got a new pair of shoes which are very beautiful, in between, he lost himself. When he had no shoes to wear he had hopes and expectations, but when he got them, many things came along; the more beautiful the shoes, the more changes occurred. I was attracted by the theme.

As for the action scenes, it was mainly due to Lau Kar-leong *[Lau also directed the action scenes on the original]* who I had never worked with before. I like to try someone new, but Mr Lau was rooted in the seventies, therefore the action scenes turned out to be quite unsatisfactory; he is still is a very good action director but the scenes he designed are just kind of old style. The action scenes, therefore, were not deliberately made that way; it was not meant to be a homage to the old films.

Can you talk about your work with Stephen Chiau Sing-chi, with whom you've made two films.

Stephen Chiao is a very talented actor and director. I first worked with him in **JUSTICE MY FOOT**, which was a remake of a thirty-plus year old Hong Kong film. I liked the original film and

杜
琪
峰

*Anita Mui and
Stephen Chiau in
Justice My Foot*

first asked Chow Yun-fat to do it. However, because of his agreement with New Cinema City Film Company, he could not do it. I then talked with Michael Hui, but he was kind of worried about the box office. Eventually Stephen Chiau agreed to do it and I thought his style of acting in this film was excellent, full of energy and life. He didn't change the script much and was very co-operative that time. It turned out to be a big movie and I moved on to work with him again.

輪廻転生の大バクチ！

周星馳
チャウ・シンチー

MAD MONK
マッドモンク
魔界ドラゴンファイター

†96東京国際ファンタスティック映画祭正式出品作品†

マギー・チャン ン・マンタ アニタ・ムイ アンソニー・ウォン
【監督】ジョニー・トー 【武術指導】チン・シュウトン
1993年／香港映画／カラー／89分 【提供】クリエイティブアクザ 【配給】彩プロ＋アジア映画社

Japanese advertising for Mad Monk

The second film we made together was **MAD MONK**, but the experience turned out to be an unhappy one. Firstly, he wanted to change the script a lot and in the process it turned out what I originally intended to say was lost. I started to lose my confidence in the film too. He affected all those who worked with him very much. Even though I never want to direct one of his films again, I must say he is very good; the number one actor in Hong Kong. But personality and acting are different things.

LOVING YOU, which I think is probably your best film, is especially interesting in that you present a very unsympathetic character in the beginning, which is quite a risk, because you still need the audience to care about his fate.

I didn't have to think about the market when I made **LOVING YOU**, because the budget for the film was only 6 million HK dollars and after making a number of films, I knew that I would, no doubt, earn back the money for the investor. Since I didn't have to think about the audience reaction, I could make the film the way I want and talk about what I like to talk about. **LOVING YOU** is one of the films I like most. It was interesting to make the audience accept the character who they dislike at first. I've rarely put scenes from real life in my films before, but in **LOVING YOU** I did; like the minute-long scene in which Lau fell asleep in his car. I experienced this in real life and I know exactly how one feels in a situation like that.

Promotional image for Lovng You

I just tried to put pieces of things that really happen in society together into the one character. It doesn't matter if he regrets his actions or not, it doesn't matter if he does the wrong things the whole way to the end, because these things happen again and again in Hong Kong's everyday life. But the most important thing is, I don't worry about the box office.

I think the film benefits from a great performance from Lau Ching-wan, who is surely the best actor in Hong Kong cinema today.

Yes, I think Lau Ching-wan is a very sensitive and careful artist; he's very imaginative and puts his heart and mind into the work. He always tries to do his best and it is most enjoyable to work with him because he doesn't do films for money. I like to discuss his way of acting with him and I kind of depend on him to make the film better. Every time we worked together, we would talk about the film all the time. We were quite happy with the outcome of **LOVING YOU**. And I have found a good actor out of it.

*Andy Lau and
Wu Chien Lien in
A Moment of Romance
Part 3*

杜
琪
峰

*You produced **A MOMENT OF ROMANCE** and its sequel, both
of which Benny Chan directed. The first film is something of a
classic, I think. But you chose to direct part 3 which was
disappointingly artificial and overly melodramatic.*

I directed Part 3 because it was more expensive and the budget
can't be less, not because I like this film. It's not very good.

*What prompted you to make **LIFELINE** and how difficult was it
to shoot?*

I made **LIFELINE** because I think people like to see films about
heroes, but I didn't want to make kung-fu films. I wanted to make
a film out of real life, so I made this story about firemen. The
slogan for the theme of the film is "Save as many as you can."
Firemen cannot save all, they can only do their best and save as
many as they can.

It was very difficult to shoot the fire scenes. We are not
in Hollywood, so we had no experts and didn't know how to
control the fire. But we, the crew, the photographer, everybody,
felt excited because we wanted to overcome this difficulty. We
did a lot of research and thought over the fire scenes very
carefully. Technical problems were not the main problem; the
main obstacle is how people overcome such a difficult situation.
I am lucky that the crew were devoted to the film and tried their
best to make the film. The risks involved in making the film were

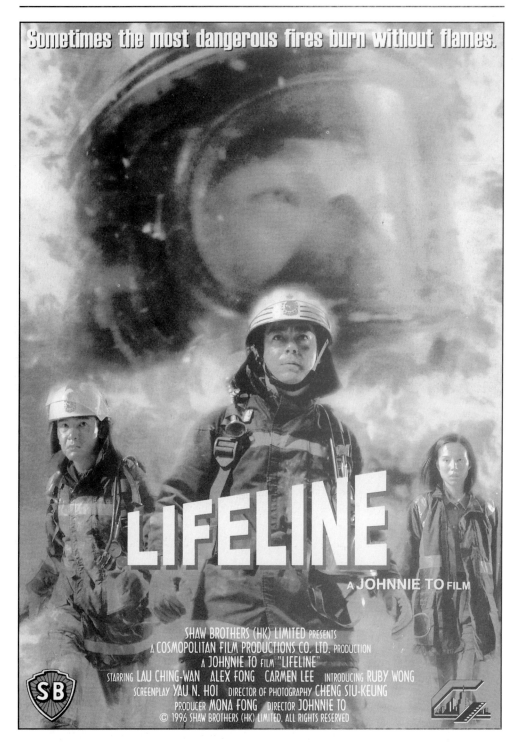

*Poster for **Lifeline***

very high but none of the crew backed out. It turned out to be great success and the whole crew should be credited for it. The production cost was only about 10 million. That's Hong Kong dollars not US dollars. The whole crew felt very honoured to have made the film at such a budget.

Lifeline

*How did you manage, on a budget that was just a fraction of that of **BACKDRAFT**, to make the fire scenes so realistic?*

It is because it is real fire! Fire is unbearable but smoke is really more dangerous and even after two months, our spit was still black when we coughed. Because it's about the life of firemen, we wanted it to be realistic, so we did a lot of research and whenever we shot a scene, we would go to the fire station and ask for the opinion of the actual firemen. We did this for nearly six months. We even stayed at the fire station for two weeks and followed the fire engine to see what it is like in real life.

You have worked in such a wide variety of genres. Are there any you prefer or do you like the constant change?

I have made a wide range of films: action movies, kung-fu movies, comedies, costume drama, nearly every kind of movie that Hong Kong produce. I am quite happy with what I have done. I am not sure what kind of movies I will produce in future, because it depends partly on the trends, what happens later, and what I think later. I may give up action movies or I may fall in love with them again later. I don't know. I like to direct movies which follow the trend and the times.

杜
琪
峰

*Johnnie To produced **The Longest Nite**,
starring Tony Leung and Lau Ching Wan*

Filmography as director

THE ENIGMATIC CASE (1980)
HAPPY GHOST III (1986)
SEVEN YEAR ITCH (1987)
THE BIG HEAT (1988) *[co-directed with Andrew Kam]*
EIGHTH HAPPINESS (1988)
ALL ABOUT AH LONG (1989)
THE FUN, THE LUCK & THE TYCOON (1990)
THE STORY OF MY SON (1990)
THE ROYAL SCOUNDREL (1991)
CASINO RAIDERS II (1991)
LUCKY ENCOUNTER (1992)
JUSTICE MY FOOT (1992)
THE BAREFOOT KID (1993)
THE HEROIC TRIO (1993) *[co-directed with Ching Siu-tung]*
THE MAD MONK (1993)
THE EXECUTIONERS (1993) *[co-directed with Ching Siu-tung]*
LOVING YOU (1995)
A MOMENT OF ROMANCE III (1995)
LIFELINE (1996)

杜琪峰

Anthony Wong

CD sleeve

Anthony Wong Chau-sang is a virtual Renaissance man. One of the most prolific actors in Hong Kong, he has also directed two films - the off-beat ghost story **NEW TENANT** (1995) and the radio station drama **TOP BANANA CLUB** (1996) - has released two CD's, and on top of that finds time to write for local publications.

The seemingly always busy Eurasian actor is one of the most popular Hong Kong performers outside his native region, due in some part to his presence in precisely the kind of Hong Kong films that many Western viewers seem to crave. He can be found in Johnnie To's 1993 super-heroine fantasy **THE HEROIC TRIO** (and its sequel), in soft-core sex romps like **EROTIC GHOST STORY II** (1991) and most notably in a host of Category III shockers: he can be seen enjoying torturing his wife in **LOVE TO KILL** (1993), as a mild mannered truck driver who seeks crazed revenge for his wife's death in the gloriously absurd Wong Jing production **UNDERGROUND BANKER** from the same year, and indulging in necrophilia and as a consequence becoming a lethal virus carrier in Herman Yau's anarchic **THE EBOLA SYNDROME** (1996).

However, this should not be seen to diminish his status in Hong Kong. He has three times been nominated for Best Supporting actor: in 1993 for Alex Law's splendid romantic fantasy **NOW YOU SEE LOVE, NOW YOU DON'T**; in Cha Cheun-yee's factually-based Category III rated **LEGAL INNOCENCE**; and, in a recurring role, in 1997's **YOUNG AND DANGEROUS PART III**. In 1993 he won the Best Actor award for his starring role in the controversial true-life crime re-enactment **THE UNTOLD STORY**.

In 1997, an offhand remark led to rumours that Wong was about to retire, but after spending several months in London taking an acting course, he returned to give one of his finest performances to date, in Gordon Chan's **BEAST COPS**. I conversed with the outspoken Wong over lunch (neither of us ate pork balls!) in Causeway Bay's Excelsior Hotel.

黃秋生

Miles Wood:
How did you get into acting?

Anthony Wong Chau Sang:
It's a long time ago, but there's a story. When I was 21 I had nothing to do, just staying at home all day. But I had a friend who had just graduated from high school who sang very well, and he was talking to me on the phone and told me I should try for the television course at ATV, which he was applying to. Anyway, he was nervous so I told him not to be scared, I would go with him. And what happened was that I got in and he failed.

So I went to the training course in 1984 for one year and afterwards I signed a contract with them for another two years. Then I went to the Academy of Performaing Arts for acting training and I got my diploma and after that went to TVB before starting my film career to become a star!

Poster for
The Untold Story

So how many films have you been in?

Fifty? I started a long time ago. I don't remember my first.

*One of the first I saw was **WUNIU**.*

Ah, **DANCING BULL**. That was a nightmare! I think it's about the personalities and I don't think Allen Fong really knows or feels what improvisation is. He wanted improvisation in every scene but for him it's a different concept. For me improvisation means you need to know the how, what, where, when, why, so that in every scene you have a goal and then improvise to reach it. He just wants you to sit down and talk and write down what you're saying and then act it out. It's not real improvisation. It's very lazy because you don't have a script. and when you get to the location you just get together with the writer.

That was the first time he'd used real actors.

Yeah. And I had a problem with the actress, Cora Miao, Wayne Wang's wife. We quarrelled and she talked to me in English, and

黃秋生

with Dolphin Chan in
New Tenant

said she didn't know how to speak Cantonese. Okay, I understand; so I told her she can speak in English and I will speak Cantonese. And she brought an English note book to the location every day, but she never read it. I was thinking she's tired or maybe she got her period!

The reviews were not very good, but he thinks he's a genius! **AH YING** was very good but maybe he just never improved himself.

Can you talk about why actors in Hong Kong seem to feel compelled to go into singing, even if they don't sing too well, and tell us of your own musical accomplishments?

黃
秋
生

Well it's not just here; there are some actors in Europe and America too. I saw in the newspaper today the woman from **THE X-FILES**, she sings! So... For me it's just for fun! Actually, I'm not interested in singing; I'm interested in writing the lyrics. But my songs, nobody sings. My lyrics are mainly about politics so maybe I've got trouble after 1997. My music is basically punk rock and also some country rock, though there's not a big audience for it. Most of those that listen to it are university students so I do treasure them. I'm proud of them.

While audiences almost expect actors to have a musical career they don't seem too receptive to actors trying to do different things within their chosen profession.

*with Yu Rong Guong in **Taxi Hunter***

They don't think, that's the problem. They don't want to think, they just want to be entertained. They don't treat you as an actor or actress; they just treat you as an entertainer. The audience doesn't know how to appreciate the films; it's from the tradition of Chinese opera. They just go to the cinema for a rest or to talk. They can't change.

Are you a star or an actor?

I'm not a star, I'm an actor, as you can see *[points to his casual t-shirt and jeans attire]* though maybe in another place I will be a star. Actually I have no money, so maybe that's the difference between being an actor and a star. You can get really big money if you're a star, and you get paid very badly if you're an actor. In Europe and America you can make money as an actor. Also, if you're an actor you have to play many different parts - a bad guy, a maniac, whatever you're given - so the audience don't necessarily like you. They just like the hero. I think they are poisoned by Hollywood films, like **BATMAN**. But I think they do respect my acting.

Western viewers, such as those in England, know you probably better than some major Hong Kong stars.

Really? You make me so happy today!

黄
秋
生

Poster for
New Tenant

Can you talk about your directing efforts?

I directed two films. One is **NEW TENANT**, the other is **TOP BANANA CLUB**. And the box office is all bad! A record!

I made **NEW TENANT** in 1994 and it's a kind-of cult film. It's about dreams: the conscious and the subconscious. I made it in 16 days - no money, no time - and when it was completed none of the cinemas wanted it, so instead of being shown three days later it took one year to come out!

TOP BANANA CLUB was made in 1996 - there were two films at the same time with virtually the same title; one is **BANANA CLUB**, mine is **TOP BANANA CLUB** - and it's about the violence of the radio station, and how the hosts on phone-in shows always cut the audiences head off, and how they bullshit everyday that they are going to solve the audiences problems. It's not the truth. How can you solve peoples' problems in just a few minutes? But the editing is not mine. It's very strange in Hong Kong. If you don't have enough power, when you end the film many other scissors come in. I'm not happy with it. They want every film to be 90 minutes. But for example, if you write a poem or a book the length is different; what's the point of cutting a novel so it becomes a poem?

Would you be interested in directing again?

Yes, I am interested, but not in Hong Kong. And I don't think they understand me, because I always come up with so many strange ideas. Here they just want you to entertain. So you have to put some jokes in your films, or some action, even if there's no point. If it's two guys talking in a restaurant what's the point of putting in action?!

*For **THE UNTOLD STORY** you won best actor award. Did this lead to a greater choice of parts?*

No better roles. Worse! All that I am offered is maniac roles. I'm tired of all those roles. I was a little bit surprised to get the award, but I think it was a political decision. In the 13th awards they wanted to make it really big, and equal, and that's why I think they gave me the award. Honestly, I did act my best, but I don't like the film, I don't like the story, because of moral reasons. It's okay, you can make violent films, but you have to put something behind them, try to say something. I was trying to do something, but for the director it was just a violent film to make money.

What is your main reason for taking a certain role?

The Untold Story

Money. Most are just for money.

Are there any you've done for other less mercenary reasons?

Some. **TAXI HUNTER**. I think that's an interesting film. It's by the same director as **THE UNTOLD STORY**, Herman Yau. We changed the script, and worked on the dialogue every night to make it more interesting. And **DREAM COP**, which is about a guy who really wants to be a cop, but can never be one. So he just thinks he is. It's a comedy and Herman Yau directed it also; he's a very good friend.

What other directors do you like working with?

Benny Chan. I've worked with him twice. The first was along time ago. A comedy with Andy Lau. It was rubbish! You know in **BIG BULLET** I speak Italian? At that time I was learning Italian and the guy next to me - the tall one with the dark glasses - is from America and he can speak Italian so he is teaching me. Well, one day when we were shooting an action scene I just shouted out some Italian and Benny came up to me and asked me what I said, and told me that it sounded good. So the next time I saw the script, my character is called Little Bird, and the line for Little Bird just said "speaking Italian." And when I asked him what I should say, he told me, "just say whatever you like"!

with Simon Yam in
Awakenings

*You're happy in a film like **BIG BULLET** to play a supporting role?*

Yes, you get more freedom. If you play the main role they have to control you every way. When you play a smaller role it's much more interesting.

*You worked with John Woo on **HARD BOILED**. Was that an enjoyable experience?*

Absolutely not! It was a nightmare! I don't think he is a particularly good director and I don't know why Hollywood thinks that he is. I think there's a lot of better directors in Hong Kong. I think he only really knows how to direct action scenes. At that time I went to the set every day - and I was working on three other films at the same time - and I had no time to sleep. And every night I went there, and I was just sitting there waiting and waiting, and eventually after several days I got to act and he told me, "You're not right!" So I said, "Okay, as a director, tell me what you want me to do," and he just says, "I don't know."

I think Johnnie To is better than John Woo. I've worked with him many times; he's a good friend and also my teacher. Sometimes you have to change your acting because in Hong Kong films the rhythm is very fast so you don't have time to "act" and then speak. You have to do it at the same time so that the director can't cut you out. And he taught me that.

黃
秋
生

***THE HEROIC TRIO**, and its sequel **THE EXECUTIONERS** are very popular in the West.*

The Executioners

That's interesting, but the make-up is so terrible! In the second one I played two roles. One of them is the Duke with long hair and I did it with a plastic mask on my face every night. It was a hard time, especially when I finish and want to go home. But I

Advertising for
Armageddon

黃
秋
生

like the films, especially the second one, in which I think the story and the music is better. Michelle, who is in the new James Bond, was very nice to work with.

She's the latest in a long line to try and break it in Hollywood. Have you been tempted?

Everyone goes to the West. Maybe I should try. But I'm not really interested in Hollywood. I much prefer British films like **PRICK UP YOUR EARS** and **THE COMMITMENTS**. And **TRAINSPOTTING**. I saw **ROMEO AND JULIET** six times; I would like to do that. And King Lear, of course!

*One of your films, **ROCK 'N' ROLL COP**, was chosen to play the London Film Festival.*

I don't think it's a good film. The story has no reason and the music was awful! Maybe they *[the Festival programmers]* don't know how to choose, or maybe Hong Kong just gave it them.

*I thought your most recent film **ARMAGEDDON** was very disappointing, but the Hong Kong audience I saw it with seemed very receptive to your performance.*

I think you're right. It took three months from the start to reaching theatres and it cost HK$10 million - we went to Prague - but there wasn't much of that for me. The audience accepts me because I play the role like them. You can see my character doesn't think too much, which is like normal Hong Kong people. They always make jokes of everything, they don't know what science or philosophy is or anything. All they know is money and sex; they sleep, work, and gamble. And that's my role. He's a fool, but he's an ordinary Hong Kong person and that's why they like him.

with Michael Wong and Sam Lee in
Beast Cops

Selected Filmography

NEWS ATTACK (1989)
WUNIU (DANCING BULL) (1990)
EROTIC GHOST STORY II (1991)
FULL CONTACT (1992)
HARD BOILED (1992)
NOW YOU SEE LOVE, NOW YOU DON'T (1992)
THE UNTOLD STORY (1993)
DAUGHTER OF DARKNESS (1993)
THE HEROIC TRIO (1993)
THE EXECUTIONERS (1993)
LEGAL INNOCENCE (1993)
LOVE TO KILL (1993)
THE MAD MONK (1993)
A MOMENT OF ROMANCE PART II (1993)
ORGANIZED CRIME AND TRIAD BUREAU (1993)
TAXI HUNTER (1993)
NOW YOU SEE ME, NOW YOU DON'T (1994)
ROCK 'N' ROLL COP (1994)
THE DAY THAT DOESN'T EXIST (1994)
COP IMAGE (1994)
NEW TENANT (1995) *[also directed]*
BIG BULLET (1996)
EBOLA SYNDROME (1996)
MONGKOK STORY (1996)
TOP BANANA CLUB (1996) *[also directed]*
YOUNG AND DANGEROUS Parts 2-5 (1996/7/8)
ARMAGEDDON (1997)
TEACHING SUCKS! (1997)
OPTION ZERO (1997)
BEAST COPS (1998)

黃秋生

simon yam

Thanks to a resume largely made up of some of the best (and some of the worst) Hong Kong action flicks and Category III pot-boilers, to Western viewers of HK films, Simon Yam Tat-wah has become a popular and frequently seen figure. Yam came to prominence when, as seemingly the epitome of cool, he stole the limelight away from his three senior stars in John Woo's master-piece **A BULLET IN THE HEAD**, and he has since lent his charismatic presence to a wide range of roles including a gay psychopath in Ringo

above and right:
Simon Yam in
Black Panther Warriors

Lam's ultra-stylish thriller **FULL CONTACT**, a deranged serial-killer taxi-driver in the exploitative **DR. LAMB**, and a hitman-turned-teacher in Joe Cheung's **THE TRUE HERO**. In 1997 he was nominated for Best Supporting Actor for his role in Raymond Li's triad drama **TO BE NO. 1**.

Yam recently saw the publication of both a picture-book and a volume of photographs he had taken, which the irrepressibly enthusi-astic and highly likeable actor proudly showed me when he found time in his busy schedule to talk to me in the office of Win's group, to whom he had recently signed.

任達華

Are your movie fans the people who buy your books?

with Veronica Yip in
Cash on Delivery

Yes, the people who like me. But also the graphic people, and the creative commercial people. Because they knew my talent. Last year I got a best talent award in Hong Kong. Only ten people were picked. They picked Kenneth, an interior designer, Peter Chan, the best director; those artistic guys. And I got a creative award, so I'm one of them. Because they knew that as well as acting, I do photography, and image work - I designed some record covers - and I've done a travel documentary by myself, going through China. So they give me an award because beside making movies I have lots of hobbies, but those hobbies are very healthy and can influence all the teenagers, and give them a good direction.

So are you interested in actually making a film?

It depends. It's another step, plus my schedule is very busy. And when I direct a film it has to be a top work. I will be very picky because I need everything to be 100% right. So there will probably be a lot of arguments between me and the artists. So I will wait two or three years.

If I direct a film it must be made in China and shot in natural light. I know films already but I have to know every department: lighting, camera, editing, props... I want a good foundation first so when I direct a film no-one can cheat me. "How can you tell me it is $500 when I know it is $200?!" I see

任
達
華

in **Expect The Unexpected**

a lot of movies from Europe, America, Hong Kong, India. I want to show why different countries have different cultures, and I want this movie to have success all over the world.

How did you initially get into acting?

When I was in secondary school I did a lot of commercial and modelling jobs.

One of the magazines influenced me a lot, but it was not a film magazine. It was a travelling magazine, and it made me want to go travelling. All around the world.

So how do you choose your roles?

I always say if you want to make a horse run fast you have to feed it good grass, otherwise, when the horse is hungry how can he run? I come from a very poor family. So in 1989, 1990, 1991, I have no choice of what parts I play. I just make lots and lots of movies; I did fifteen or sixteen a year. Before that I was at TVB. In most of these I was the bad guy. But in these last two years I'm able to be more selective, and only do five or six a year. But I got my income.

If the role is small but the character is good; even if it is only 5 minutes. I was nominated for **TO BE NO. 1**, even though I act for only 5 days. Because I love acting. I'm always saying I'm

with Anita Yuen in
Crossings

not a big star. I'm an actor and I would love to act in different types of film, in all kinds of roles. This makes me more happy. Since I have money and lots of property I can pick all those pictures where the character is good. So I refused **REPLACEMENT KILLER** because the role is no good. I don't mind playing a bad guy but I need to show *how* the bad guy is. It was nothing. It cannot make you a star because the role is bad. When I first act in America I want to at least give people some talking point.

Do You want to act in Hollywood?

It depends. I don't mind trying. I made **CROSSINGS** in New York, though it's a Hong Kong production and very low budget. As long as they give me something to do. If they give me opportunities I will go. But if not, there is no point for me to wait in Hollywood for two or three years. If I work in Hollywood I can easily adapt to the culture, because I know everything; I know how to act in America, because I know the culture very well. So there will be no need to wait for two or three years. Although my English is not perfect, simple English I know. I learn all my English from TV!

You've made a lot of action movies.

So why does Simon Yam make a lot of action movies? It's the only way easily to make communication between people from

任達華

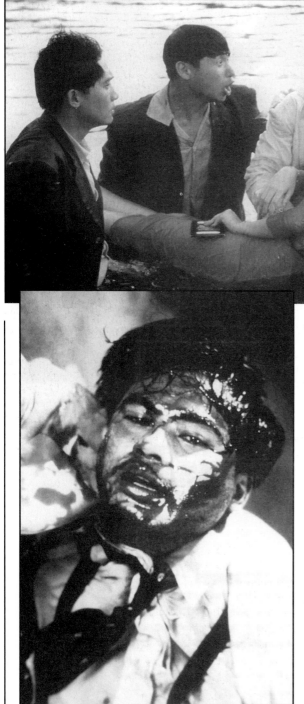

*two dramatic scenes from **Bullet in the Head***

different countries even though they don't understand the culture of those countries.

When you make comedies or love stories they don't understand what it means. They can't fill in the culture, especially the tradition of Chinese. It's totally different for American people. That's why sometimes I will act in American style and sometimes in local style. To please the local market. To please the South East Asia market.

When I act in a Japanese movie I have to exaggerate a little because they like that. So I do a lot of research. Even if I make a lot of low-budget films, I can still survive. Of course, I like big-budget film, but I have to survive. But if nobody pick you... At the same time when I get the script I will always do my best. Which is why low-budget producers pick Simon Yam. I always say that some actors and actress are unfair to producers of low-budget. For example, in Hong Kong we often make lots of films at the same time and they will always give all their days to the big-budget

with Linda Wong in
Police Confidential

film. It is unfair to them. I will not be like that. Everything is equal: you cannot say because the director is good you will give all your time to him. Even if on the low-budget film the script is not so good I will try to make it more active.

What film first got you noticed?

BULLET IN THE HEAD... and **FULL CONTACT**. I was disappointed with **BULLET IN THE HEAD**; I like John Woo, he's a nice guy, but when the movie came out they didn't get me to do any publicity; when the Korean producer wanted people to go and do publicity they didn't pick me. I don't know why. I never touch alcohol and don't hang round with people who drink, but this is Chinese society and they need someone to go with them and drink. I thought in that movie I acted very well and if they'd put me forward in the promotion maybe I could become a big star. It made me very disappointed and quite depressed but also made me more determined to try to do everything. You can't just rely on luck. So I make a lot of movies and make a lot of money.

For **FULL CONTACT** I created a lot of elements inside that role; I added a lot. The script was basically just Simon Yam and Chow Yun-fat, so I told Ringo we should make it that he loves the Chow Yun-fat character, and when he refuses him, I

任達華

with Carina Lau in
Gigolo and Whore

want to kill him. It makes the film more complicated. This is life; this is human beings. I insisted that they thought about it for about two days and they said okay; so Ringo is a very good director. He is very open, very receptive to your ideas. You can talk to him.

Are there any other films that you've made that you're particularly fond of?

I've made almost one hundred movies and I'd say every one is good... Some Americans don't understand the culture, so **FULL CONTACT** and **BULLET IN THE HEAD** are a little more like European or American movies, but I can't say that they're the best because most of them, such as **HONG KONG GIGOLO** or **GIGOLO AND WHORE** are for the Chinese market, for Hong Kong and Singapore and Malaysia. So I can't say which is the best. It depends on the country and the culture. All the girls are crazy for me and all the boys are jealous! I can't really say **FULL CONTACT** is the best because it's for a different market, a different culture. **CROSSINGS** is very good, but it's not suitable for the Hong Kong market; it's suitable for maybe the Chinese market or the American market. And the Singapore market; because my acting is not exaggerated. In Hong Kong you need it to be very fast. So I act in different style for different market.

Many people say to me "don't make action movies" but I say, "Why?" They can communicate. The reason I am very

with Cecilia Yip in
Love, Guns & Glass

popular in China is because they saw a lot of my action movies. They don't understand comedies or love stories but they like action movies. I've been walking around China and Tibet and Mongolia and everywhere they like me and it's because of my action movies. Unfortunately they're copies, it's not the original, but I don't mind. It gives them a chance to watch me. A month ago I was in China and it was very poor, and they just set a TV on the street and they are just watching my film; even if it is five years old they still like me. Film is about communication. So when I'm asked to stop for one year to make artistic films I say "No." Hong Kong is instant noodles, no culture. So why make artistic films; they don't understand them. That's why they like Hollywood films.

The most important thing is I know how to act. I will try all types of roles to give me good experience. Like **DR. LAMB**, some of those psychopaths. I wrote a script last year in Singapore and acted as a mute. I stopped two movies in Hong

任達華

above: Poster for
Killer's Romance

opposite top: in **Dr. Lamb**
opposite bottom: Poster for **Dr. Lamb**

Kong because this was different for me, and I wanted to try it. It's like Dustin Hoffman in **RAIN MAN**. Sometimes you have to have that kind of experience.

*You made a film in England called **KILLER'S ROMANCE** which successfully transposed the Hong Kong action formula to another part of the world.*

A lot of people like that, because the fighting sequences are so exciting. I like it. I didn't use a stunt man. I normally did all the stunts myself. I said I wanted to try it; to get that experience. Go Fei is very strong guy, so I used a pad and all my energy. Although it was painful I wanted to feel it. When I was in England people would recognise me, especially a lot of black guys, and ask me for my autograph.

貪污舞弊的大時代 一羣與惡勢力鬥爭到底的英雄

絕不低頭 FIRST SHOT 出品人馬碧蓮 監製導演林德祿 領銜主演狄龍 張曼玉 任達華 李子雄 劉錫明 許志安

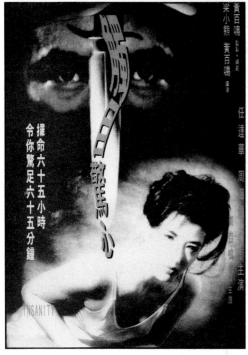

top:
Advertising for
First Shot

above:
Poster for
Insanity

Selected filmography

FATAL TERMINATION (1988)
TIGER CAGE (1988)
BURNING AMBITION (1989)
BULLET IN THE HEAD (1990)
KILLER'S ROMANCE (1990)
BLACK CAT (1990)
BULLET FOR HIRE (1990)
GIGOLO AND WHORE (1991)
POWERFUL FOUR (1991)
QUEEN'S HIGH (1991)
CASH ON DELIVERY (1992)
DR. LAMB (1992)
FULL CONTACT (1992)
NAKED KILLER (1992)
INSANITY (1993)
HOLY WEAPON (1993)
LOVE AMONG THE TRIAD (1993)
ROSE, ROSE I LOVE YOU (1993)
RUN AND KILL (1993)
BLACK PANTHER WARRIORS (1993)
A DAY WITHOUT POLICEMEN (1993)
CROSSINGS (1994)
THE TRUE HERO (1994)
LOVE, GUNS AND GLASS (1995)
MAN WANTED (1995)
POLICE CONFIDENTIAL (1995)
TO BE NO. 1 (1996)
STREET ANGELS (1996)
YOUNG AND DANGEROUS Parts 1-3 (1996)
HITMAN (1998)
CASINO (1998)

yim ho

Yim Ho

Yim Ho is one of Hong Kong's most Internationally recognised film-makers. After studying at the International Film School in London, he returned to Hong Kong in 1975 to work in television. Breaking into films in the late seventies, his approach is notable for the fact that he has worked in China five times using mainly local crews. **HOMECOMING**, *which delved into the roots of Hong Kong people in through a woman returning to her native village in Guangdong, won six awards at the 4th Hong Kong Film Awards and was later voted best film of the eighties by Hong Kong film critics;* **RED DUST**, *a truly moving drama in which Brigitte Lin gave one of her finest performances as Shanghai writer Eileen Chang, won eight awards at the Taipei Golden Horse Film Festival;* **THE DAY THE SUN TURNED COLD,** *an atmospheric murder mystery cum morality play was voted best picture at the 1994 Tokyo Film Festival; and the little-seen* **THE SUN HAS EARS** *won the jury prize at Berlin in 1996.*

Yim Ho was interviewed in the poster gallery of the 1997 Hong Kong Film Festival, which his film **KITCHEN**, *a style-conscious adaptation of Banana Yoshimoto's novel, had opened.*

嚴
浩

The Day the Sun Turned Cold

嚴浩

Miles Wood:
You've worked there so often, many Western people are under the impression that you're actually from China.

Yim Ho:
Although I was born in Hong Kong I do go back and forth to China quite often. I went there with my mother, brothers and sisters when I was a kid because we had relatives in China, and I've returned quite often in the past ten years.

What are the constraints of working in China?

When you work in China you have to be very aware of the different set of rules that apply to film-making. For example, you must not make films that upset the Government. In a way it's not unlike America, where they have politically correct groups, who make sure people aren't upset, but there it comes from civilians. In China it comes from the Government who make sure you do not upset the juridical system, the Police - every policeman has to be a good policeman! - or the birth control department, whatever. Of course, they have their reasons, not just political ones, but because these people, who are all like individual organisms, will complain and then the censors will themselves face criticism. So you have to be careful no-one gets stepped on.

How valuable was your time spent in London?

Siqin Gaowa in
Homecoming

England was an important experience, but in a social context rather than a filmmaking one, because it was the first time I was truly exposed to Western culture, and that really broadened my mind in many different aspects. As for filmmaking, I was introduced to many great movie-masters; in fact, four of them I would say helped shape my style: Buñuel for his surrealism in film: Jansco, the Hungarian director, for his staging, Ozu for his powerful simplicity, and Coppola for his complexity.

After which you returned to Hong Kong and worked in television.

That's right. I was working in TVB as a writer, producer and director for three years, and then I started making my first movie, called **THE EXTRAS**, which is a comedy. I made three movies before **HOMECOMING**, which was really the turning point in my feelings towards filmmaking. I was beginning to shape my style and I was also growing up as a person, so those films represent some of that process.

*Can you speak about **BUDDHA'S LOCK**?*

BUDDHA'S LOCK, which refers to a lock of hair, was based on a true story about an American pilot who was shot down during the anti-Japanese war, and unfortunately he landed in their tribal mountains, where they have never seen a white man before, and so since he has blue eyes and blond hair they all think he must be different from a human being! So they kept him as some kind of creature as well as a slave, and he spends ten years there before eventually he's discovered and rescued by the military.

*Chun Han and
Brigitte Lin in
Red Dust*

After that I was gathering my strength trying to decide which direction I should take, because for me, filmmaking is the self-reflection of my own state, both mentally and psychologically, the way I think of life. And so all these films were done rather unconsciously. For example, **HOMECOMING** is a rather sad movie because at the end the characters are left quite helpless, and it seems like fate has controlled them totally. And again in **BUDDHA'S LOCK** and **RED DUST** the characters are totally entrapped by their environment. And actually, I think that was my attitude towards fate at the time, that people were predestined by fate.

*What exactly is your contribution to **KING OF CHESS**?*

I spent a hell of a lot of time, energy, and effort turning the two books into one script, and somehow in the middle of it, Tsui Hark, who was the producer of the film, got paranoid. In the beginning of Tsui Hark's producing career - a few years later he confessed this to me - he was too hot-headed. Even filmmakers have to go through a period of coming of age, becoming mature. At that time I think he was not too organised and the film was taken out of my hands and so only those parts of the film in which I actually appear are shot by me. And the other parts were shot by Tsui Hark. It's all in the past now.

*Was it a personal interest in Eileen Chang that hat prompted you to do **RED DUST**?*

嚴
浩

Tony Leung Ka Fai in
King of Chess

RED DUST is a very, very emotional film and because of that it's not a very well balanced movie. The only reason I made it was my emotion towards the June 4th crackdown, and so it turned out to be maybe too emotional. Brigitte Lin was very good, but actually, I don't think I've worked with a difficult actor or actress so far.

息子の告発

1994年東京国際映画祭　[京都大会]グランプリ・監督賞

愛が欲しかった。

少年はいつも母親をみつめていた。
忘れることのなかった父の言葉。
10年の歳月を越えて息子が問いかけたのは、
愛なのか、それとも真実か……
中国安徽省で実際に起こった事件をモデルに
描く衝撃の問題作。

嚴浩(イム・ホー)監督・脚本作品(原題・天国逆子)
THE DAY THE SUN TURNED COLD (1994)

*Japanese advertising for **The Day the Sun Turned Cold***

You said earlier that fate plays an important part in your films.

There comes a change with **THE DAY THE SUN TURNED COLD**, where the characters are trapped not only by their environment but also by their own frailties, the human weakness. So they should be responsible for their own fate. Then there comes a total change in **THE SUN HAS EARS** where the leading character is a woman who rises from being a very humble peasant and is able break away and control her own fate. I was in the middle of writing the script and realised I'd found something more challenging. So **KITCHEN** is no longer about fate; it's about coming of age, it's about healing, it's about the impermanent existence of human beings where death is simply a part of life.

Unfortunately the message is mostly expressed through visuals and in a way is quite Oriental, and very few Western critics have been able to detect it. It just struck me that most Western critics are not very sensitive to subtleties in Hong Kong and Chinese movies, or else they have preconceptions with Chinese movies. When they watch a Chinese movie they want to see what they want to see, for example, a perverted man who is abusive and has many wives and is cruel to animals, or else they want to have a political undertone which, of course, is anti-Communist. And if they don't get these two elements it's as if they've gone to the wrong supermarket.

I was telling friends as a joke that I was glad that Picasso was not born Chinese because first of all he'd be shot by the Chinese Government because his paintings were so corrupt and anti-traditional, and second he'd be murdered by Western critics because they just want to see that slit eyes and flat nose, and that kind of brush painting style, and if they don't see it they say it's trash. I think critics have their own standard of judgement for Hong Kong films, so it's difficult to get applause if you do something different.

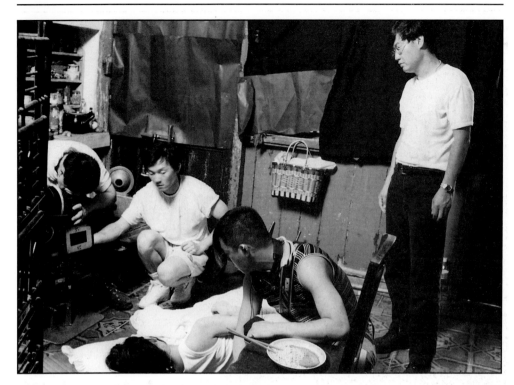

KITCHEN *was a Japanese co-production with a Japanese star.*

Yim Ho directing
Kitchen

The reason I cast the Japanese girl *[Yasuko Tomita]* even though she's playing a Chinese character, is that I saw her performance in **CHRIST OF NANJING**, where she also played a Chinese character and was so convincing. I just fell in love with her immediately, and knew she would be perfect for the role in **KITCHEN** because she has a face which is sweet and sad, and has a delicate appearance and it's all very suitable for the role. It turned out she worked very hard, and in the film she spoke Cantonese phonetically, which meant she had to memorise every syllable, and was quite incredible.

Were you forced to make any concessions for the Japanese market?

The Japanese producers were very co-operative, leaving everything in my hands, and I was able to do anything I thought was suitable for the film. I don't think I'd do anything different to suit one market, because I believe my films have to have qualities which can be appreciated by different people from all different countries and cultures, so although you need a passport to go into a country you shouldn't need a passport to go into a movie. That is what I believe.

Did you encounter any problems in adapting the novel? You changed the setting and the viewpoint.

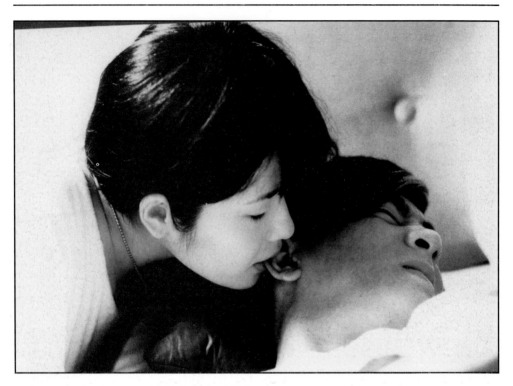

Yasuko Tomita and Jordan Chan in **Kitchen**

The story was universal and set in a metropolitan city and all I really needed to change were the names and some of the eating habits, such as the characters eating sushi. The viewpoint was not changed because of the cultural differences but because I thought it would make it easier for the audience to understand the message in the film. So it could be related filmically instead of being hammered home.

Was it a conscious shift from a female to a male perspective? Many of your earlier films are centred on women characters.

In **KITCHEN** both the young man and the young woman are important but in some of my previous movies like **HOMECOMING** and **RED DUST** the lead characters are female. Well, probably psychologically, I'm very fond of women so I do like to see them in my films *(laughs)*, and I think in a film where the main character is a woman, you are able to probe deeper into the psychology of the person, because women are more sensitive I think, more emotionally vulnerable, and so there is more room for drama. If the main character is insensitive you end up focusing more on the characters around them instead.

Music always seem to play an important part in your films. You've used Otomo Yoshihide several times.

I'm very sensitive to the music in my films. I always pay a lot of

attention and give very, very strong opinions to my composers, for example, what the tunes shall be like, or what sort of atmosphere should be created, and what instrument arrangements should be like. So I work with them very closely.

What do you perceive for the future of Hong Kong cinema?

I don't think there will be much change in a short time. The Chinese Government have their priorities and the Hong Kong film industry has never been known for its politics. Hong Kong films are always escapist. So, if we keep on making escapist movies nobody will get hurt. Lu Ping, in fact, the highest official in China who's responsible for Hong Kong, did say nothing will change in the Hong Kong film industry. He was referring to the Category III films, and he actually said, "After '97 you can keep on making them, and if you want you can even make Category IV or V movies." So we are now planning to make Category VI movies!

But I really don't honestly know, because this is the first time in history a capitalist system is going into a communist system. It's always been the opposite. Judging from the economic preferences and open policy of China, I don't think they want to shut Hong Kong down, because it does nobody any good.

top and above:
Yasuko Tomita in
Kitchen

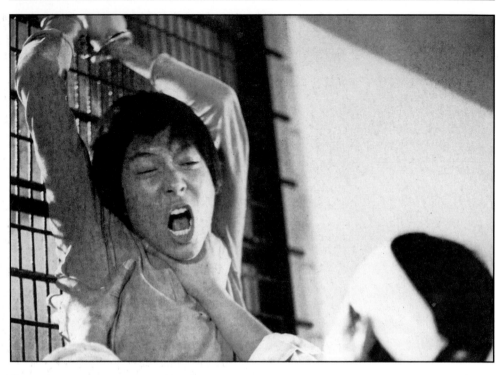

Happenings

Filmography:

嚴
浩

THE EXTRAS (1978)
HAPPENINGS (1979)
WEDDING BELLS, WEDDING BELLES (1980)
HOMECOMING (1984)
BUDDHA'S LOCK (1986)
KING OF CHESS (1988)
RED DUST (1990)
THE DAY THE SUN TURNED COLD (1994)
THE SUN HAS EARS (1995)
KITCHEN (1997)